MARJORIE WARKENTIN

SAYING YES TO LIFE

EMBRACING
THE MAGIC
& MESSINESS
OF THE JOURNEY

This is a work of nonfiction. Any resemblance to persons living or dead should be plainly apparent to them and those who know them, especially if the author has been kind enough to have provided their real names. All events described herein are all true from the author's perspective.

The content of this book is for general instruction only. Each person's physical, emotional, and spiritual condition is unique. The instruction in this book is not intended to replace or interrupt the reader's relationship with a counselor, physician, or other mental health professional.

Copyright © 2020 by Marjorie Warkentin

All rights reserved.

Printed in the United States of America.

Editing by Amanda Johnson
Cover and interior design by Caitlin Pisha
Photos by Marjorie Warkentin
Author photo by Catherine Beerda-Basso

ISBN 978-1-7344265-2-6 (paperback)
ISBN 978-1-7344265-3-3 (ebook)

Library of Congress Control Number: 2020900937

Published by Awaken Village Press, Sioux Falls, SD
www.awakenvillagepress.com

SAYING YES TO LIFE

EMBRACING THE MAGIC & MESSINESS OF THE JOURNEY

MARJORIE WARKENTIN

PRAISE FOR *SAYING YES TO LIFE*

"This book takes the reader on a journey of self-discovery, inviting each of us to remember that the simplest path in life will always be found with a conscious connection to your true self."

— Bronwen Sciortino, simplicity expert and international author of three books, including *The Economy of Enough*

"One woman's inspiring journey toward self-actualization and self-determination."

— Joanna Bergen, feminist and human rights activist

"*Saying Yes to Life* provides a unique guidebook for trails that women will encounter from young to senior adulthood. The writer has a way of taking the unfoldings of ordinary life and gleaning wisdom from them. She recognizes that many women struggle to put their true desires into words, and she seeks to model this trail of self-care and courage. A joy of nature grounds this book in beautiful landscapes."

— Janet E. Boldt, mentor, educator and business owner of Madrona Mentoring & Soul Care

"Beautifully written, this is a heartfelt companion and guide to women in times of transition and the book to pick up when life isn't going the way you want. This book is like sitting down with your wisest girlfriend at her kitchen table; warm, honest and wisdom-filled. When you get up to leave, you know you will never experience life in quite the same way as before. *Saying Yes to Life* is a book about living courageously, leaving the reader feeling that being who you are is the greatest adventure of all."

— Amy Biondini, energy healer and shaman

"*Saying Yes to Life* takes the reader on a journey of self-discovery, inviting each of us to remember that we are the leaders of our own lives. An antidote to burnout, overwhelm, and chronic stress so many women are experiencing today, each path is an invitation to liberate the Wise Woman, discover more of our true authentic selves, and open to receive the abundance of life."

— Cathryn LeCorre, MEd, leadership coach and educator

"'Know thyself' comes to mind as Marjorie Warkentin explores what it has meant for her to live into her personal journey of self-discovery and becoming better acquainted with the inner workings of her heart and mind in *Saying Yes to Life*. In her usage of metaphors of nature and hiking the trail, she invites each of us to join her in the magic of exploring our own pathways."

— Edythe Neumann, friend and lover of books and trails

"*Saying Yes to Life* is a book about the rugged and sometimes trying journey to self-trust and ultimately self-love. For those of us who identify as people-pleasers, rule-followers, or 'good girls,' Marjorie shows us how to bravely examine this deep-rooted identity and tap into our own inner wisdom with curiosity. Her stories of self-doubt, restlessness, and exhaustion are familiar tales of many women today. *Saying Yes to Life* serves as a trail guide for readers to navigate those feelings and find their own path to hope and acceptance with an invitation to stop and enjoy the view along the way."

— Cristin Connelly Zegers, life coach and aromatherapist

"I love a story where people survive life and come out the better for it. *Saying Yes to Life* is just that and celebrates the miracles that happen when one follows their heart."

— Kathy King, practitioner of traditional Chinese medicine

"Using narrative ideas and practices, Marjorie Warkentin courageously protests the dominant 'expert' stories of family and society which tend to inhibit and constrain women's personal development. *Saying Yes to Life* articulates the 're-authoring' of Marjorie's story through the discovery of her inner wisdom, personal values, and authentic expression. This creative and sensuous narrative provides a helpful guide for the traveler who chooses to embark on a journey that brings forth the inner wisdom of the 'emerging woman.'"
— Evangeline Willms Thiessen, MAMFT, DMin; systemic family therapist and clinical supervisor

"Full of personal stories and insights regarding inner transformation, *Saying Yes to Life* is bound to inspire and awaken the hearts of many as they walk their own journey."
— Cathy AJ Hardy, retreat facilitator and spiritual director

"*Saying Yes to Life* is a book about the embodied feminine. Marjorie Warkentin helps lead us back home to ourselves through her stories of trust, surrender, compassion, and listening to our inner knowing. This beautifully written book takes the reader on a journey of self-discovery, inviting each of us to remember our inherent worthiness and majesty."
— Alison Lee, coach who helps clients remove the veils of who they think they are to discover their unique, pure, bright Essence

"Reading this book is to experience a tremendous gift. With intimacy and vulnerability and by digging deep, Marjorie peels back the layers of her life and generously offers the wisdom she has gleaned along the journey—confusion to clarity, fear to strength, and pain to joy. Beautifully written and transformative, *Saying Yes to Life* is a journey you will not regret."
— Rhonda Nicholls, writer

"In *Saying Yes to Life*, Marjorie Warkentin generously shares insights from her own life's journey. She inspires her readers to be open to the wisdom that each of us holds within ourselves. This book is especially valuable to readers who are at a time of transition in their lives."

— Margaret Archibald, women's circle participant

"Marjorie's honesty, courage, and wisdom flow through each and every sentence of this book. After reading, I felt nourished, inspired, and deeply connected to my Intuition and Inner Compass. The book is a must-read for anyone desiring to live authentically with peace and purpose. Her story is accessible, relatable, and deeply moving. I am applying her tips for gracefully navigating life changes, and I feel much more trusting and supported. Thank you Marjorie! I will be re-reading this book for the reminders and insights going forward. I say YES to life with you!"

— Cora Poage, heart whisperer and life coach

"In *Saying Yes to Life*, Marjorie Warkentin provides the reader with the steps she consciously takes as she seeks language and understanding of the developmental journey that we are all called to make. The author clearly articulates ownership of those choices, attitudes that she embraces, and ultimately acceptance of the outcomes that come with these chosen pathways."

— Lorraine Isaak, long-time Readers Group friend

"This creative narrative flows from Marjorie Warkentin's soul. As I read *Saying Yes to Life*, I laughed out loud, shed tears for her inner child, and found myself pondering many things she wrote. The reader will get out of the book what is needed for them in that moment of their life. They can pick it up again many months or even years later and different

sections will likely speak to them. This is a manual for life, not a book to read once and put on the shelf."
    — Samantha Stevens, manager British Columbia Health Authority

"A beautifully written book about the author's journey from a woman who manages to a woman who thrives. *Saying Yes to Life* offers clear insight into the gifts available when you pay attention to the 'whispers of wisdom' within while engaging in a dialogue with the inner critic which tends to quiet that voice. This book left me feeling hopeful about the abundance of life even in the midst of messiness."
    — Sharon Klassen, long-time friend

"This book takes the reader on a journey of self-discovery, inviting each of us to embrace not only the uncertainty but also the wonder of the life path we are called to walk."
    — Maryann Jantzen, retired English professor

"*Saying Yes to Life* takes readers on their own spiritual pilgrimage as we recognize our backpacks are heavy, are inspired to discard the superficial, follow our 'inner compass,' and embrace the journey of discovering our own authenticity."
    — Sharon Dueck, a fellow pilgrim

"What a compelling read! Marjorie's style of weaving intriguing personal stories with profound insights drew me along to the finish. It is packed with practical guidance that one can implement immediately into their own life. This is the kind of book that is to be read again and again. Can't wait until she writes the next one!"
    — Dr. Mary Lou Riederer, optometrist

"*Saying Yes to Life* takes the reader on a journey of self-discovery, inviting each of us to remember that our desires matter, that we are living stories, and that our inner wisdom is our inner compass always guiding us to where we need to go."

— Camila F. Márquez, life coach who specializes in embodiment, creativity, ancestral connection, and self-love, and host of The Catalyze Podcast

"Full of insight and wisdom, *Saying Yes to Life* offers the reader an opportunity to awaken and trust their intuition so that they can live from their personal power and deepest wisdom. Warkentin expertly weaves her teachings, storytelling, and personal experience to create a captivating journey of self-discovery and transformation. Reading the book feels like coming home—coming home to the self, to truth, and remembering why we are really here. Warkentin's warm spirit, vulnerability, and authenticity infuse the book with a relatability that feels like having a conversation about life with a close friend."

— Rush Dorsett, voice empowerment coach and founder of Embodied Voice Coaching

"*Saying Yes to Life* inspires me to re-awaken the relationship I have with my inner wise woman. Marjorie shows us how living a life rooted in following our heart's guidance creates the most abundant life experience possible. Her writing feels honest with elements of joy and play. She shares stories at every stage of life, offering wisdom along every part of the journey."

— Kelley Cooper, life coach

"*Saying Yes to Life* is a beautifully written journey that allows the reader to be present through the messy process of weeding through the roles and behaviours we adopt to feel valued; ultimately finding the authentic self through listening to inner wisdom. As I read this book, I was struck by how each path we are taken down has relevance in different roles and relationships in my life. There is something for everyone regardless of age, occupation, or personality to support growth and a new appreciation for our inner wisdom."

— Dr. Lindsay Adrian, ND

"*Saying Yes to Life* feels like a gentle stroll in nature with a trusted friend. Guiding you inward with both wisdom and vulnerable experiences, Marjorie's loving voice is a powerful reminder of our own magic! Each chapter empowers you to journey deep within and emerge as your truest self."

— Orly Levy, life coach

"This story of a journey from caution, obligation, and dependency to curiosity, adventure, and a YES to life is everybody's story. This book is a useful reminder of what is possible for us all."

— Peter Block, speaker, consultant, and author of *The Answer to How Is Yes* and *Community: The Structure of Belonging*

"Reading this book feels like the author is holding out her hand inviting you to join her on a walk. She shares intimate learning through her life experiences and points out truth-like tall trees along the path. Her questions become your questions. At one point, you peek over and notice that the author's Wise Woman is walking beside her, holding her other hand. By the end of the book, you glance sideways to happily confirm your own Wise Woman has been there holding your hand the whole time as well!"

— Rita Kampen, lover of words and wooded areas

I AM A WOMAN

"I am a woman who came through the darkness into the light.
I am willing to be vulnerable and share my story.
I ask for help.
I ask for what I desire.
I say yes to unreasonableness.
I am feminine flow.
I dance in the spaces of trust and surrender.
I trust myself and my body.
I am sensual.
I feel everything fully: gratitude, sadness, joy, and anger.
I am acceptance.
I am worthy to be celebrated.
I am play.
I am loved.
I am love.
I am whole."

— Marjorie Warkentin, aka Wise Woman

TABLE OF CONTENTS

Praise for *Saying Yes to Life* v

I Am a Woman xv

Acknowledgments xxi

Preface...xxv

Introduction xxxi

Prologue: Hiking With My Wise Woman 1

Following the Leader 5

Finding a New Guide 17

Emerging.. 33

TRUST 47

    Make Friends With My Inner Critic 48

    Receive With Joy 51

    Expect Abundance 56

Take Risks 60

Choose Responsibility 63

UNCERTAINTY 69

Embrace Chaos 71

Await Unexpected Gifts 75

Be Present 78

Accept What Is 81

Surrender and Let Go 85

AUTHENTICITY 91

Feel My Feelings 93

Release Shame 97

Practice Self-Compassion 100

Care for Myself 103

Embrace Play and Pleasure 106

LEADERSHIP 113

Find the Gift in Everyone 115

Face Fear 117

Be Strong and Fierce 121

Set Boundaries 123

Stay Committed.. 127

True Belonging 135

Epilogue: A Love Letter From My Wise Woman.... 145

References 153

ACKNOWLEDGMENTS

This book and my heart are filled with gratitude to the many people who have touched and inspired me.

As I reflected and wrote my life story, I was struck by the love and generosity that met me at every turn. I may not have seen it in the moment. However, I see it now from my current vantage point.

I want to take this opportunity and start by giving thanks to those with whom I have interacted throughout all these years and who may not even know the influence they have had on me. Thank you. I also want to acknowledge my gratitude for those who have more specifically played a role in the writing and creation of my book.

Thanks to my son-in-law who challenged me almost a year ago. He asked me: "Isn't it time to stop talking about writing a book and just start writing?" And that is what I did!

Thanks to Amanda Johnson, my editor and book doula. Amanda and I met in a life coach training program and nurtured our friendship over the next four years. When I was ready to write a book, Amanda "just happened" to have a business that offered editorial support for aspiring authors. She has been an integral part of my book writing journey. We laughed, cried, and created together as I embarked on my path to becoming an author. Lightness and love kept us company, and because of her brilliance and wise editorial guidance, I am now able to offer you my first book. I am deeply grateful to you, Amanda!

Thanks to my coach, Alison Lee. Because of her coaching, I was introduced to my Wise Woman. Alison has been a mirror for me as I deepened into my self-awareness and learned that it is possible to trust myself rather than defer to the "experts" in my life. Many of the ideas and phrases used in my book are taken from the words I heard my Wise Woman say during my coaching sessions. Alison wrote down the messages I received, which I humbly share with you, my readers.

The cover design of my book is a result of a magical collaboration. My friends Art and Sharon Dueck gave me a T-shirt with a beautiful artistic wild woman on the front. This inspired my brilliant designer, Caitlin Pisha, to create the cover that conveys my Wise Woman inviting the reader to "Say Yes to Life." Thank you, Art and Sharon, and Caitlin.

ACKNOWLEDGMENTS

My family has been walking beside and supporting me the entire way. Thank you to all of you for your patience and cheerleading! And, specifically, to Al, my husband, who never stopped believing I could do this.

My book is a reality because I have been supported beyond my wildest dreams.

PREFACE

Writing has always been a way for me to reflect on what is happening in my life.

When I was ten, I got a diary with a lock and key. Every day, I'd write down what I did—more often the facts than my experiences of them. Even then, I was keeping track of what was happening to me. Even then, I had a story to tell.

I recall sitting at my desk in grade four, eagerly waiting for my creative writing teacher to give us our writing topic for the day. The class had quickly become my favourite time of the week. I loved imagining the scenes my teacher suggested, lost in another world as I considered the words to describe what I saw in my mind's eye. She told me I was a good writer. Her words and belief in me encouraged me and kept me going. When our family went on road trips, I would sit in the back seat, writing in a notebook, pretending I was writing letters to faraway imaginary friends. I had a feeling of excitement, happiness, and fun in this world I created.

As I grew older, I wondered if I would ever write a book. But my life was full and exciting. I worked full-time, raised my three children, and then welcomed their children into my life as a grandmother. Writing a book didn't enter into my plans again for many years.

When I enrolled in a life coach training program after I retired, I started writing blog posts for my website. I was reminded of how I'm an observer of my life and how I notice patterns and ways of being that I would miss if I didn't stop and reflect. The joy of creating my world around me and playing with words resurfaced, and I wondered again, Would it be possible to write a book?

My writing is a process that supports me in gaining clarity, listening to my inner wisdom, and then taking action based on what emerges from this reflection. As I write, I focus on the gifts in my life and get to know myself more deeply. Much like the ten-year-old who wrote letters to her imaginary friends and created worlds in which she could enjoy the pleasures of life, I now see how writing gives me the same permission to create the life I want to live by reflecting on where I have been and where I want to go and seeing the next steps to make it happen.

Writing is a way of "coming home to myself."

Decades after the first impulse and a few years after the second inkling, I was once again called to write my book. It was a deep longing that yearned to be expressed—both for me personally and as a way of sharing my gifts with others.

Even though I knew I was on the right path, I felt a mix of emotions. I was excited and anxious. Suddenly it all felt messy, and I was filled with uncertainty. How does a book get written? Where would I start?

Evidence that I was aligned in my life showed up for me when I connected with a coaching colleague who "just so happened" to have a business as a book doula and editor. I knew working with her would be a joyful process and that I would relate to her way of communicating. Amanda and I had known each other and talked regularly for a few years, and I felt at ease in our friendship.

PREFACE

As I started on this new path of writing a book, I longed to have this sort of partnership. I could taste the deliciousness of having an editor support and encourage me. I had a sense this was the direction I was being led.

Then reality set in.

How could I afford this type of support on my budget? I had my pension cheque, which covered our living expenses and not much else. My heart sank, and I felt the crushing weight of disappointment in my body. I experienced dark sadness in my soul as I brushed off my ambitions thinking it was a ridiculous dream anyway.

I cried. I wrote in my journal. I went for a walk in the woods. As I allowed myself to feel my feelings, I wondered if I could find the money somehow. Uncertain and a bit nervous to discuss it with my husband, I took that first step.

What happened next was magical.

My husband, Al, was aware of my calling to write. He had heard me share my deep desire to work with Amanda. He read her proposal, and I waited. My heart was racing, and my palms were sweaty. I wanted to trust that whatever happened would be for the best. I wasn't sure what that might be.

Al finished reading the proposal and was quiet for some time. Then he said, "We can do this. We'll find the money."

I could hardly believe my ears. Tears in my eyes, I told him how happy I was and how thankful I felt for his support. We looked at our finances and, together, saw a way to pay what was required. It would take sacrifice and some hard choices. We agreed they'd be worth it.

The experience gave us a sense of partnership and risk-taking that deepened our love for each other. Al's humour stayed intact through it all. As we completed that initial conversation, he playfully assured me, "This is all possible. As long as there is a book at the end of it all!' I laughed joyfully and held him close, declaring, "Yes, there will be a book! There's no doubt in my mind about that."

I paid the first installment and began my weekly calls with my editor. I knew I was on the right path, and I celebrated my courage in taking a step toward writing my book.

Shortly thereafter, my husband's parents called the family together to celebrate their 70th wedding anniversary and new home. They'd sold their previous place and moved into a smaller one where they'd receive extra support. What a surprise when my father-in-law gave each of his children an envelope. What was this? It wasn't our turn to be celebrated.

The magic happened again.

My husband's parents had chosen to gift us with an early inheritance gift. We opened the envelope. It contained a cheque for the exact amount of money I owed my editor.

I was speechless. Abundance had shown up in an unexpected way. What a beautiful affirmation of my choice to write my book and to trust I could say yes to this dream. What a significant sign from the universe that my needs would be supplied. What evidence that my faith had been rewarded.

PREFACE

Before I saw a clear answer to my needs, I trusted. I took a step, and the path before me appeared. I had been given the money I needed in order to proceed. I had a deep longing and clarity about my desire to write a book, and the universe heard and supported me. I wonder, had I been less sure of what I wanted, if abundance would have shown up in such a way.

My parents-in-law were thrilled when they heard how the money had come at such an opportune time for me. They were curious about my book, and I noticed the connection we felt as I shared my book-writing journey with them. I received with open arms, and they experienced joy in turn. It was what I call a true gift exchange—we all benefitted from the gift.

I have a story that I have been given to share with others. It's bigger than "my story." It's a life-giving fountain. And it is my responsibility to write, trusting that those who are thirsty for it will find it.

Saying yes to life is something I practice each and every day. And, as I pause and write about my life, I see that I have been doing it for some time.

I invite you to join me.

— Marjorie Warkentin
February 26, 2020

INTRODUCTION

In my conversations with women, I hear a longing to live life more fully. As I share my experience, insights, and life learnings, I realize I have wisdom to offer these women, who are eager to hear more and apply what they receive to their lives.

For most of my life, I inhabited what I describe as my masculine energy. I faced obstacles and pushed through at all costs. I didn't trust my intuition. I was too nervous to think for myself. As a result, I deferred my decision-making to the experts in my life.

I was skeptical of my body. I didn't believe it had anything worthwhile to tell me. I felt a secret sense of shame in its beauty, sensuality, and power. I'd been taught that my faith was separate from my body, that I needed to overcome its "sinful desires."

I was panicky at the idea of "letting go" emotionally, particularly apprehensive of what I perceived as "dark" emotions. I saw myself as weak if I cried or showed fear or anger, holding back my self-expression for fear of disapproval. I was full of fear. Worried thoughts tormented me: Am I good enough? Did I do the right thing? I derived my identity from being a helper to others, my worth always tied to what I accomplished. My motivation was always to act in ways that would please others, especially authority.

As we travel along our life paths, we spend a lot of time with our noses in the guidebooks, staring at maps drawn up by others and trudging ahead despite the conditions we perceive. We lose touch with our inner compass and miss out on the beautiful vistas, the hidden treasures along the way, and many trails that lead us to unexpected places.

When we follow our inner compass, on the other hand, we may pause, listen, or even take the river downstream. There's a creativity that happens when we're not stuck to a rigid map or method. We see other options and are willing to take risks to try them.

For much of my life, I've loved hiking. My husband and I even went hiking on our honeymoon. We've since gone on family hikes with our children and grandchildren. It doesn't matter that these days I'm usually at the back of the pack. I love the feeling of anticipation at the beginning of the trail, wondering what will be around the next turn in the path. I'm struck by the parallels between the journey of life and the experience of hiking.

This book is a portrayal of the journey of how I travelled from a place of the heavy obligations I discovered at an early age to a heart-centred life filled with lightness and love. Even when I had no idea where I was going, I learned to look up and enjoy the view or slow down and splash in the puddles.

There is no specific guidebook for this adventure called life, no one way to reach our destination. In fact, it is the journey itself that we will be paying attention to rather than pushing through to "get there" and missing the beauty along the way.

There is a lot of wisdom revealed by paying attention to the little things. These little things—the events I call the nitty-gritty of life—add up to the big things. Nothing is too insignificant. I've come to see that small happenings create the possibility of new future experiences we don't

INTRODUCTION

even know about at the time. Whether during a trip to the dentist or unexpected car trouble, my life lessons come from transforming my experiences on a daily basis.

There will be times for revelling in the messiness of life's questions and playing in the mud and other times for ascending to a variety of viewpoints and resting spots. Taking these trails, we'll lighten our loads as we go. I used to carry so much in my backpack—fears of what others thought, rules passed down to me from authority figures in my life, advice from all the experts. The lessons we learn as we get rid of the beliefs and habits we no longer need will allow us to travel light, as I now tend to do.

I am alongside you to witness your journey. Trekking together, I sometimes follow your lead, pointing out paths you haven't yet taken. Doing so, we traverse new territory and reach new viewpoints and vistas. As a result, you are supported so you can create a life that is filled with purpose and joy. I am committed to our finding the wisdom that is already within you.

As I take you, my reader, on the trails I explore in this book, I invite you to notice how I've been guided by my inner wisdom. Each step has been divinely orchestrated whether I knew it or not.

You will see that it's possible to live a life filled with love and grace. You can trust yourself and learn to listen to your intuition. You will no longer need to depend on external guidance or approval when you come to a crossroads. You will discover the benefit of stopping and paying attention to what your body is telling you, listening to the messages within. You will learn to differentiate the voice of your inner wisdom from that of your inner critic. You will come to experience the peace that results from trusting yourself and moving forward with confidence.

Our first trail invites us to inquire: What does it look like to trust myself? We'll traverse all sorts of terrain including a secluded spot for us to meet that quiet voice inside that has so much wisdom. There will also be the chance to make friends with the nagging inner critic, so we can more confidently explore the concept of receiving the abundance that will support us on our hike toward self-trust. This comes at a great time as we will need this reminder when we are then asked to take risks. That's certainly not my favourite path. I tend to face it with the anticipation of a drop-off or a huge boulder to somehow climb over. Together, though, we will be inspired to see risk-taking in a different light as we hike along and encounter what it means to take responsibility.

We embark on another trek along a trail marked with the sign-post "Uncertainty." The path itself is a mess, obscured by brambles, roots, and fallen logs. As we trudge ahead, we see what appears to be chaos. Believe it or not, the best way to navigate this trail is to keep going rather than avoiding it. When we see it as part of our journey and embrace it, chaos loses its power over us.

It helps to look at this as an adventure. There is the possibility of fun and play even when we aren't sure where the trail is leading. As we take our time and pace ourselves, we see the tiny mushrooms under a log and catch sight of small animals scurrying off as we step along. When we pay attention to what's around us, noticing the wildflowers and the amazing shades of forest green, we tend to forget about the rough trail beneath our feet.

The next trail claims it will lead toward discovering how to live authentically. As we walk along, we learn it's okay to admit when we're feeling exhausted, fearful, or upset and why that admission is healthier than pushing our feelings down and *pretending* everything's

INTRODUCTION

okay. In addition, we are asked to face our shame, despite not wanting to go there. From this more authentic place, we are prepared to explore the importance of caring for ourselves (not only thinking of others' needs), practicing greater self-compassion, and experiencing more play and pleasure while splashing around in a glacier-fed pool that rejuvenates us all.

With newfound energy and clarity, it's time to dry off and begin our quest toward "Being a True Leader." Right away we'll discover that everyone has a gift and that it's not only the person in front who's the leader. We all are. This does not save us from stumbling onto a dark and treacherous-looking side-trail that winds its way across our path and asks us to face our fears. We must remind ourselves that in order to become strong and fierce in our power, we need to check this one out. This invites us to set boundaries, removing resentment and self-pity from our backpacks. Just as we are getting tired and wanting to turn back, we are asked to be committed to our journey in spite of the rough patches we've encountered.

Put on your hiking boots and prepare to join me on these trails. Don't delay—the weather is perfect, and, I assure you, you won't be disappointed in the experience. You'll find treasures along the way and make many memories to keep you going after the hike is over. Who knows, you may even choose to invite others to accompany you on these trails when you return for more adventures.

As I take the path of saying yes to life, I embrace the magic and the messiness of it all. Now, I am true to myself, and I follow the inner wisdom I have access to. I invite you to join me on this messy path of adventure full of magical experiences.

Prologue:

HIKING WITH MY WISE WOMAN

》》———→

I'm on a trail in the mountains of Waterton Lakes National Park in southern Alberta, Canada. The sky is blue, and the air is crisp and cool. It's late summer, and there's frost at night. The leaves are beginning to turn colour. The weather grows warm by noon, and I'm able to take off my jacket and tie it around my waist. The path climbs upward, and I enjoy the wild blueberries along the trail. I pace myself and stop to look at the distant mountains surrounding me.

My Wise Woman is not easy to see. She is a shadow in the cluster of birch trees. Just when I think I've caught up to her, I see her loose-fitting, flowing pants, her top billowing as she floats higher up the trail. I hear the gurgling of a mountain stream. When I stop by the stream for a lunch break, she is reclining against the moss-covered rock. She smiles warmly and welcomes me with a musical, loving tone. She has a colourful backpack playfully decorated with a silver bear bell and sparkly stickers. She wears comfortable boots and a soft, woollen shawl in a rich, red colour. Her long dark hair is cascading around her shoulders, and she seems just fine with the bits of grass and twigs caught in the curls.

After my lunch, I lie back in the sun and close my eyes for a moment or two. When I open them, she is gone. I smile to myself and know she will not desert me. It's almost as if she and I are hiking independently, and she trusts that I'll call on her when I need to. I am not worried. I have come to trust her deeply.

The pine trees are sighing and swaying in the wind. Suddenly I feel a shower of raindrops. I look up and see the mischievous wink of my Wise Woman as she disappears into the dark clouds that have suddenly appeared. I grab my rain jacket and pull my hat down over my ears. I stay in the circle of the pine trees until the rain eases off.

Then I see the hint of a rainbow across the valley. My Wise Woman has changed into a sparkling robe of purple and vivid orange, and she calls to me from a bluff high up ahead. Is she in the rainbow? Or is that her on the bluff?

There's a stand of blackened trees from the forest fire several years earlier. As I walk past the desecrated area, I catch a glimpse of new growth. There's a splash of red against the black. My Wise Woman is nestling in amongst the ashes, encouraging the tiny flowers to keep growing. Her loving, feminine energy is life-giving, and I breathe it in for myself as I keep trekking along.

I stop for another break at the bluff. There she is, sitting cross-legged on a patch of soft leaves. She holds out her hand and offers me a piece of dark chocolate. We sit together and savour the delicious mix of sweet and sharp bitter flavours. I lean against her shoulder, and she hugs me gently. She whispers, "You are safe. You are following your own wisdom, and I am here to celebrate your trust in yourself."

My eyes fill with tears of joy, and I take a deep breath as I snuggle into her embrace. I am exactly where I am meant to be. I can relax about what comes next, knowing that I am strong and capable. And that I am not alone.

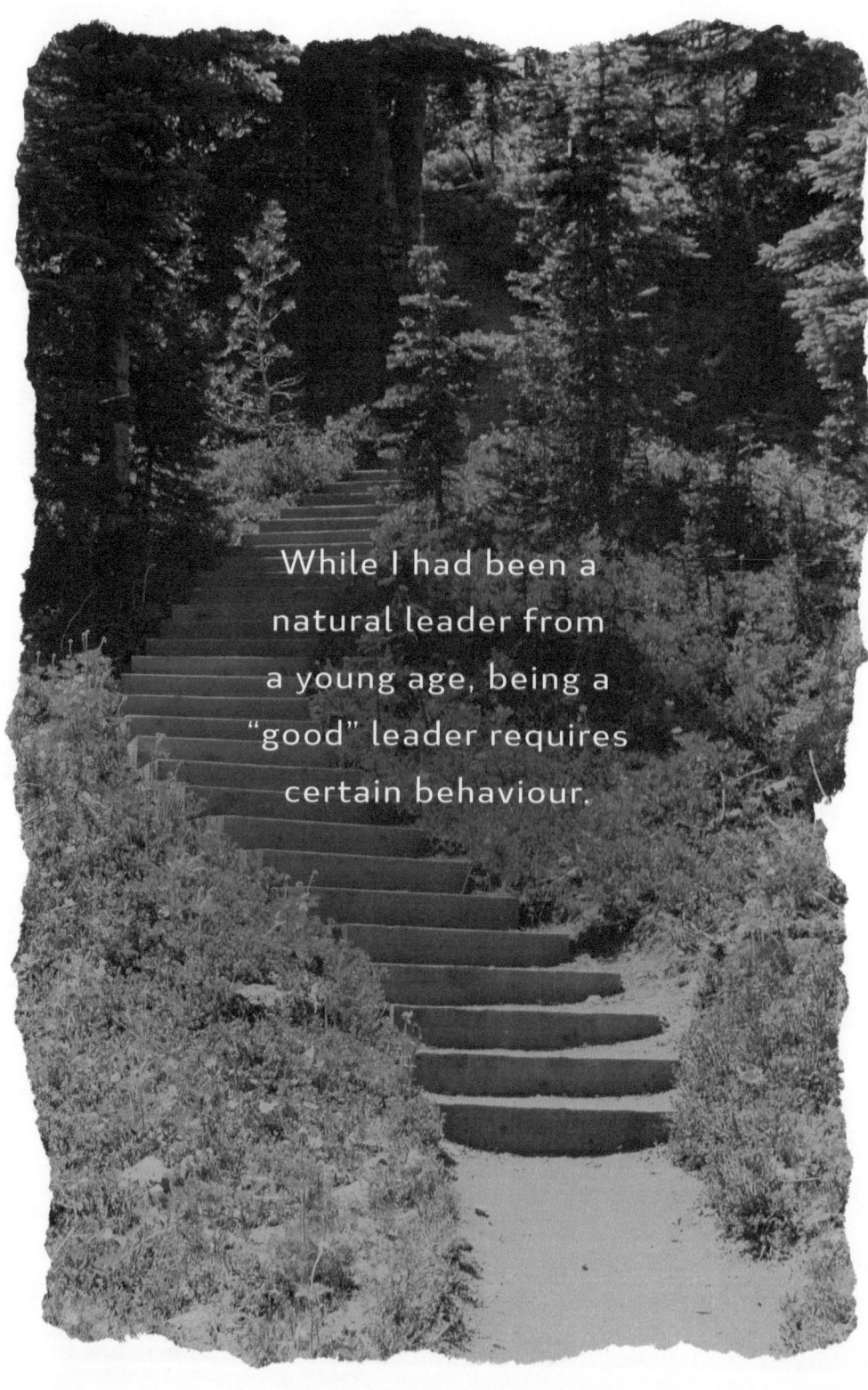

While I had been a natural leader from a young age, being a "good" leader requires certain behaviour.

FOLLOWING THE LEADER

≫⟶

I was ten years old when my mother and I went to visit a woman in our small prairie town who was sick and lived alone. In those days, people like her were called shut-ins. I felt sad just hearing that word. Shut-in. What would that be like? I sat quietly while my mother visited with the woman. I looked around and wondered what life must be like for her. I saw her helplessness as she sat in her chair. She seemed unhappy as she looked down at her hands, folded in her lap. She appeared tiny and frail under the shawl that was wrapped around her shoulders. I wondered whether there was any fun in her life. The house seemed crowded with dark furniture and cluttered with papers and dishes. No toys, no pets, no music playing, no open windows to let in the fresh air of an early spring day. I was glad when we finally left.

As we walked home, I said to my mother, "I hope my life doesn't turn out like hers." My mom stopped and looked me in the eyes. "You have a choice about that, Marjorie. Your life doesn't have to be like hers at all. It's up to you what your life is like." And we kept walking.

What did my mother mean by that? Could I really choose what my life would be like? Did I have the power to do that?

I was born and raised in a preacher's home, where it was taken for granted that I would follow the instructions given by a Higher Power. As a young girl, this meant obeying my parents without question. I didn't even consider the possibility of going against what my parents told me to do. There was an emphasis on doing the "right thing," and, wanting approval, I accepted my role as the obedient daughter.

As I grew older, I learned more about the teachings of the church and other voices of authority. I remember thinking it was too scary to say what I wanted because I was sure it wouldn't be the 'right choice' for me to make. Chances are I would be in trouble if I followed what I desired. When I said I didn't want to babysit my younger siblings or if I listened to the Beatles on my transistor radio, I was scolded or grounded.

I internalized a message: I am not wise enough to trust myself. I had to trust in a higher authority and perform the correct actions in order to earn love and approval. I had no concept of being loved for who I was. Still a young girl, I wanted to feel secure in my home, and the only way I knew how to feel safe was to do as my parents said. I didn't know of any other options. I yearned to be told I was a "good girl" and worked hard to make sure I did what I needed to be accepted. Hoping to be perfect, I pressured myself to keep at it without stopping.

I also had this approach at school. I was competitive and determined to get top marks, working hard to be the leader in the class. One day, my grade four teacher announced she hadn't yet finished marking our tests—the results would be ready a day late. The delay frustrated me, eager to know how I'd done. Raising my hand, I complained, "Oh, you'll probably say the same thing tomorrow." She went quiet and dismissed the class, calling to me on my way out. "Marjorie, I'd like to speak with you."

My heart seemed to stop, and I struggled to breathe. Oh, no, what now? I knew my comment had been sassy, and I just wanted to run away. She looked at me with an expression that surprised me: sadness. "Marjorie," she told me, "you're a leader in this class. The other students look up to you. They think what you do is the right thing to do. Do you want the way you talked to me to be how the others act?"

I shook my head no, and she went on to encourage me to act in a way that would be a good example. I hadn't received a scolding. I hadn't been shamed. I'd been challenged to act differently. I was intrigued by this idea of being a "good example."

It became clear that, while I had been a natural leader from a young age, being a "good" leader requires certain behaviour. No more rude comments to my teacher. Be kind, even when I'm mad at someone. Put others' needs first. Lead according to external rules and norms, and do what was right in other people's eyes.

I wasn't encouraged to ask questions or discuss other options when it came to certain behaviour. Why did I have to care for my younger brother when the rest of the kids could play? Why couldn't I go to school dances? What was the problem with rock music? I wore long dresses and loose-fitting pants instead of mini skirts and jeans like my friends were wearing. I longed to be like my friends yet wanted to be accepted by those I viewed as experts, seemingly in charge of how life should be lived. But I didn't complain. I kept my anger inside. I was a big girl. I was the helper. I had to be a grown-up. I didn't have temper tantrums like the young ones who cried when upset. I was too old for that. I stifled my feelings and did what was expected of me. I would watch the adults around me, hoping to learn which behaviour might please them, lacking the ability to make decisions on my own.

Sadness and anger were feelings I never knew I could express. Instead, I would shove them down, thinking I wouldn't be loved if I showed my negative emotions. Giving in to others' demands without complaint was necessary if I wanted to be liked, so I would smile, comply, and carry on. I didn't know there was any other way.

The few times I did make my own choices, I was told I could do better. I loved to read, and at the age of twelve, I decided I was ready for more interesting books. I checked out a romance novel from our church library. When my father saw me reading it, he took it away, claiming "those kinds of books" weren't suitable for me. He didn't say why. All I knew was that I'd made a bad decision.

Following my own desires always seemed to lead to trouble.

In the summer, I enjoyed playing ball, running on a dare across the pasture where the nearby farmer's bull was kept, and building forts in the tall grass of our crabapple orchard. I wore pedal pushers and enjoyed the comfort of not wearing a dress. One day I came to the supper table wearing them. It was another bad choice. "Go change into a dress," my father demanded, explaining that I was a girl and should dress appropriately. Even my piano teacher disapproved of my actions at times, rapping my knuckles with her ruler when I made a mistake and telling me I hadn't practiced enough.

We moved to a large city when I was thirteen. I stood before my new class in my shiny brown shoes, so different from the other students' running shoes. The teacher introduced me: "This is Marjorie. She's a top student, and I'd like you to give her a warm welcome." My cheeks burned bright pink as I looked at my new classmates. They were in jeans and t-shirts while I wore a vest and purple plaid skirt that was the outfit mandated by my parents. Their long, straight hair made me aware of how short and curly mine was. I wanted to disappear.

After school, I rushed home, careful to cover my fear and anxiety with the brave face I put on. I grabbed my diary from the bedroom I shared with my sisters and wrote about my awful day. And then, as usual, I carried on in the hope of pleasing others, wanting to belong in this new world and doing everything I could to get through this challenging time. My friendly smile hid a hurt I had no words for. I said no to being myself and admitting the hardships of my life. When the other girls refused to lend me their study notes, I kept quiet. When I was teased in gymnastics, I hid my tears. My reaction was always to work harder and please others the only way I knew how.

By the time I turned seventeen, I had adapted to life in the city. I loved my friends and the many opportunities my school offered. I found a love of and aptitude for sport when I joined the badminton league. I took part in *The Pirates of Penzance* with the glee club, an artistic community whose sets, costumes, and music introduced me to a whole new world of creativity. I was working on designing my prom dress in sewing class. My biology teacher inspired me to learn more about my new favourite subject. My boyfriend and I were talking about a possible future together. I finally belonged.

And then I got the news. We were moving again, now to a small town several provinces away. I was devastated. I said goodbye to my friends, careful to hide my heartache as I tried to convince them that the move was for the best, and followed my parents' plans for me.

Once again, I was the new girl, joining a close-knit graduating class of only twelve students who had been together since grade one. A big-city girl who shared no history with my classmates, I was treated with suspicion. With entirely new school subjects and teachers, I even struggled academically. There was no sewing class, glee club, or biology teacher in this small town. My boyfriend was hundreds of miles away.

I rushed straight to my bedroom after school. Finally alone, I could cry—but only for a few moments. I pulled myself together, saying no to my deep sense of loss. Instead of admitting to it, I distracted myself with long hours of study and tried to make the best of things.

This technique seemed to work as a way of coping with change and loss—do what is expected of me, and all seems to be well. I joined the church choir and participated in the school drama, though it was nothing like it had been the year before. My situation was hopeless, it seemed.

I had no experience paying attention to my inner desires or expressing sadness and, therefore, no insight into what I was really going through. I wanted to move back to Calgary, and I felt constrained and depressed. I was stuck, so I had to make the best of it. I was in the habit of pushing away my dreams of what I wished could happen. It was a coping mechanism and an attempt to accept my life as it was, but it kept me from feeling the pain and loss of what I no longer had.

Even then I intuitively knew there was something I didn't relate to in this new place. I desperately wanted to fit in and belong, so I ignored my inner turmoil and would go to parties and events that didn't really interest me. I continued trying my best to act in ways that would please the new people in my life.

Because I had spent so much of my life following the rules and expectations of others, I struggled with believing in my own ability to make choices that were for the best. At the same time, I was resentful about always doing what was expected of me. When I did listen to my inner wisdom, I saw it as a rebellious act. I felt guilty and worried I would get caught. I was in a tight spot—unhappy following the advice of the experts and too afraid to trust myself and step out on my own.

But I craved independence and started testing the limits. I went out with friends in the evenings and got home past curfew. I went to school dances, telling my parents I was in charge of playing the records when I'd actually be joining my friends on the dance floor. Alone in my room, I listened to the music that appealed to me. I spent time with schoolmates who weren't from my church and had intriguing dinner table conversations in the company of families with different values from mine. I saw an acceptance of a variety of ideas and a willingness to ask questions and even disagree about certain issues. I was becoming aware of a different way of showing up in life.

When I graduated from high school, I embraced my newfound independence by moving several provinces away from home. I enrolled in a Bible college, a traditional, conservative school that closely resembled the values of my upbringing. I still felt the push and pull of wanting to follow my desires and feeling the pressure to obey the rules.

On the outside, I mostly fit in as a young woman who acted as expected. Underneath, I was questioning things and starting to take chances at following my desires. My approach was different now—I'd think twice about blindly following norms. I was learning to assess what I wanted to do, taking small steps toward self-trust.

I knew early on that I wanted to be a nurse, and I was not going to give up on my dream. I've always taken pride in being a hard worker, focusing on the tasks that need to be done and the goals I want to reach. I've driven myself to be the best I can be, no matter what else is going on. I was drawn to the idea of having a career and being independent, even if many of my friends were more interested in marriage and the security of finding a husband.

As I started taking action based on my own conception of what is best, I got a sense of what it's like to create the experiences I want. I knew it was up to me to figure life out—I wouldn't have parents or teachers with me all the time. What an adventure that realization was. Sometimes I was excited and moved ahead with ease. Other times, I wondered what I was doing and slipped back into following others' expectations of me. After completing two years at the college, I moved to Winnipeg and embarked on my dream of becoming a nurse, preparing to start a nursing course in the fall.

But it was early summer, and I needed a job until then. The previous summer, I worked at a care facility for developmentally handicapped adults, many of whom were unable to communicate and needed full care. It was stressful and tiring with long hours and challenging working conditions. I wanted a summer job that was less depressing and demanding. It was a risk to look for a new job at this point, but I had begun listening to my inner wisdom. I heard what my heart and soul wanted and decided to take a chance.

I applied for the role of nursing care aide at the Winnipeg General Hospital. I knew the working atmosphere would be more positive and supportive. I successfully made it through the interview, and, then, I was told I didn't get the job because I was only available for a few months of work.

I looked at the woman who had interviewed me. "I'm going into nurses' training this fall; that's why I'm not available after September." I felt let down, but I wanted to be honest with her and clarify that I had a valid reason for my time constraints. I thought to myself that I should have pretended I'd be able to work longer, just quitting when I needed to. I heaved a big sigh, wondering why life is so hard before I realized she was still talking.

"Where will you be studying?"

"Here, at the Winnipeg General Nursing Program."

She went quiet and looked at me with a smile. "What size uniform do you wear?"

I was speechless. I knew intuitively that this position had been prepared for me even before I'd known it was possible. I left the interview with lightness in my heart. It was one of the first experiences in life that showed me I was being led. I had trusted in myself, and look what happened. I was assigned to the maternity ward unit, full of life-giving and joyous energy. What a gift!

Learning to listen to my inner wisdom has been a lifelong journey. It started before I had the words to describe what was happening. Looking back, there were times when I responded to the quiet whispers, when I was drawn to read a new book or talk to a new friend. Yet there would still be many more years of ignoring what my inner voice and body had to say. Sometimes I did say no to an activity I didn't want to do, but it wasn't an easy task for the girl who loved to please and make others happy.

As I reached my early twenties, I learned how to manage my life with increasing levels of success. I was capable of handling most of what life threw at me, not realizing that there may be more ways of doing so than the method I had employed for so long. I still found myself ignoring the impact of a sad event or acting as if it really didn't bother me. My boyfriend and I broke up, yet I didn't cry. Telling myself it was for the best, I didn't allow myself to feel the deep loss of my reality.

I had no concept of the process of emotions moving through me, nor of the release they could result in. I didn't know what it was like to really grieve. I continued to pay attention to what would please others in my life, wanting to "get things right." No matter how exhausted or discouraged I felt, I ignored my body's messages. I treated a headache with Tylenol and tiredness with more coffee. I learned to live with a tightness in my shoulders and a stomach that was often unsettled. I rarely let on that I was worried about the future. I coped by pretending and hiding my anxiety.

Back then, I didn't know the term "numbing." I didn't recognize that eating a whole bag of chips or several cinnamon buns could have anything to do with my mood. I didn't understand the relationship between my body and my emotions. What I did know was that I could manage my feelings of anger, sadness, and fear by keeping busy. When I worried about not being able to control how others perceived me, I distracted myself. I pushed through despite my exhaustion, ignoring what my body was trying to tell me, saying yes to helping others even when I wanted to say no. Furiously cleaning the bathroom, running as fast as I could on the trails, or planning a social get-together were perfect distractions so I could ignore my internal disconnect and carry on with my life as I knew how.

FINDING A NEW GUIDE

›››———▶

Weary, constantly questioning whether I was on the right track, I put on a brave smile and survived each day, pretending everything was okay. I continued living according to what the supposed experts in my life had told me. As long as I followed their ideas, retained their approval, and was seen as a good leader, all would be well.

My life kept on like this for many years, and I was married with young children by the time I realized there might be another way. I met people with different spiritual beliefs who followed their own ideas and desires. They challenged the rules and didn't seem to worry about appeasing authority or a narrow view of life. I was curious. How were they able to live a life of freedom without feeling guilty?

This was a crucial time for me—I could no longer ignore my soul's calling. I was being introduced to new ideas and started to question much of what I was taught as a child. I realized there were other ways of thinking about life and many of my long-held traditions no longer met my needs. I used to feel lost unless I was involved in a variety of church activities. Teaching Sunday school, singing in the choir, and attending all the services were ways in which I found security and identity. As I developed interests outside the church and found friends that welcomed me into their circle, I saw that the church was only one way of being in community.

I read books that encouraged me to think independently and led me to analyze my faith. Books such as *Mere Christianity* by C.S. Lewis and Richard Rohr's *Everything Belongs* expanded my view of the Divine. From there, I was led to books that inspired me even more, including *Gift from the Sea* by Anne Morrow Lindbergh, where I first glimpsed the possibility of spending time with myself and getting to know who I really am, deep down inside, and Jean Vanier's classic, *Becoming Human*.

In my reading, I was told that I had wisdom and could trust myself rather than looking up to the "experts" I'd always counted on. This was a new concept for me—such a rule-follower who didn't often think for herself—and I felt some trepidation as I considered leaning on my own intuition. What if I got it wrong? What if my choice displeased others?

The thought of displeasing the experts who had guided my life up until then created a new kind of anxiety that I had to confront. I felt nervous and restless and wanted to know what to do next. I began therapy sessions and discovered parts of myself I wasn't even aware existed. I saw how I put myself last when making decisions. I saw how eager I was to please my father, repressing any of my ideas or emotions that might upset him. So much of my life had been focused on how to keep him happy.

After several sessions, the therapist asked, "Don't you think it's time to take your father off the pedestal you've put him on?"

I was stunned. It sounded sacrilegious to me. How could I be so disrespectful?

I felt afraid. My therapist and I talked about how I could start making choices from my inner wisdom and learn to trust myself. What might that look like? What would be next? All I knew was that I could not keep on with the way things were. I was no longer willing to continue living a life based on making sure my father was pleased.

It was a pivotal step for me. My father was only human, a realization that radically changed my perspective on our relationship. He had his beliefs and values, and it was time for me to choose my own. There had been something in it for me to want so desperately to please him all these years. He was doing the best he could do, and so was I.

This is a significant stage in one's personal development, and I took longer than some to break away from my family's way of doing life. I had been afraid to openly rebel as a teenager. Then, in my early twenties, I accepted that this was the way life was—not really questioning any truths or thinking for myself, blindly following what I had been told all my life. Finally, in my early thirties, I was ready to do the work of differentiating from my father and other authority figures in my life. I started thinking for myself and making choices based on what I wanted. It was a time of trying on new ways of being, and I had many moments of wondering if I was doing the right thing.

I had grown up with a lot of fear—of displeasing those in charge, of my own body and what it was capable of. My body and its desires, I had been taught, was something to be suspicious and wary of. I didn't realize my body had messages for me based on my innermost wisdom. I hardly knew I even had this inner guidance and was hesitant to accept that I was good enough just as I was. My worthiness had always been contingent upon what I had accomplished and whether others approved of me.

With the help of my therapist and friends, I began to hear the whispers of my inner wisdom. I began to act based on what I wanted rather than what pleased others. I no longer blindly followed those I saw as experts.

Here is what I came to realize: God doesn't disapprove of my listening to my inner wisdom. In fact, God is the one who gave me a soul that knows what is best for me. He (or She) is smiling at the path I am on and the joy I have in trusting myself, knowing that I don't need experts to guide me.

It was a rocky trail to traverse, but I kept going. At times I stumbled or was misunderstood. I doubted myself and felt the temptation to go back to my old way of making choices. I caught myself reverting back to linking self-worth to accomplishment and measuring my success by my capacity as a helper and leader. It seemed like I was on a trail consisting only of switchbacks and not moving forward at all.

I was the family's major wage earner for many years. It was a choice my husband and I had made when our children were young, both being committed to having one parent at home with them as much as possible. Al and I met in Saskatchewan at the Bible college we attended right out of high school. Four years later, I said yes to the adventure of marriage with him.

By my early thirties, we had been married for twelve years and both changed quite a lot during our time together. We were shifting away from a more traditional depiction of marriage and were willing to experiment with alternative choices in our relationship in ways many people didn't understand. It was the early '80s in a conservative town, and a father staying home with the kids was an unorthodox choice.

That's just what my courageous husband did, though. He stayed home with our three children, ages seven, five, and two. I accepted a position as a nurse in critical care and gave it my all. Long shifts, overtime, and ignoring my body's needs became the norm for me. After all, I was the one responsible for our family's financial situation. What would happen if I didn't keep going?

Even with all I was learning, I refused to imagine that life could be any less stressful. Friends of mine had the summer off and often went to the lake or on road trips. I told myself that that kind of life wasn't for me. I was destined to be responsible and work hard without breaks, so I ignored my feelings of sadness and self-pity and immersed myself in my work. I thought that denying my feelings of jealousy would make it easier for me to cope with my life. I was stuck in my role without even a glimmer of light that anything else was possible.

I've always taken pride in being a hard worker, focusing on the tasks that need to be done and the goals I want to reach. I've driven myself to be the best I can be, no matter what else is going on. Even as a young woman, much of my identity came from this aspect of my personality.

All these years later, my identity remained linked to my accomplishments. Before I went to sleep, I made mental lists of what I had done that day, ranking my self-worth accordingly. I consistently fell short of my high standards and wondered if I could ever accomplish it all. In turn, I slept poorly and woke up overwhelmed, neither eager nor excited about the day ahead. Troubled with doubt and unrest, I started to wonder if there was more to life.

I ignored the occasional whispers of my inner wisdom. Still wanting to please those in authority over me, even if I was tired and depleted, I would drown out the meek voice by distracting myself with hard work, food, and helping others. Despite the books I had read and what my therapist had shown me, I kept pushing myself in order to get things done and receive approval from others.

Until my body finally got my attention.

After years of putting pressure on myself to appear competent and successful, I was exhausted. I was entering my fifties, and there were many changes in my body. My energy was sluggish. I would feel blue and start crying for no apparent reason. On top of everything, I was on a mission to get in shape and lose some weight. Even with a careful diet and exercise plan, I gained weight. That's not how it's supposed to be! I was floundering in a swirl of sadness and self-loathing. No matter how hard I tried, it was a barrier I couldn't seem to push through. My life was a mess. My relationship with my husband was suffering. I had no interest in nurturing our marriage. I saw myself as a failure. Why would my husband want to be with me? I withdrew into myself, staying in bed for long hours even when I was unable to sleep.

Who was I becoming? All my life, I had enjoyed a healthy body and an emotional state that was, for the most part, positive and upbeat. I longed for the time when I'd wake up with a zest and curiosity for the adventures the day might bring. Would I ever feel happy and energetic again? I worried there was something seriously wrong with me. I didn't want to live this way anymore. I needed help.

Finally, I saw my doctor. Struggling both physically and emotionally, I swallowed my pride and asked for help. After a series of blood tests and a visit to a specialist, I was diagnosed with an under-functioning thyroid. I took the pills prescribed and waited to feel better. I kept waiting. Nothing seemed to change. I was still tired and discouraged. It seemed there wouldn't be a quick fix.

Along with taking the medication, I was told to slow down and take care of myself. Me? Slow down? It was something I was good at telling others to do, but I had a different standard for myself—I could push through without a break; I was strong. Except now, everything had changed. I was no longer able to manage the way I used to.

I knew I would need help to understand what slowing down meant. I was ready for my life to change. The next time my inner wisdom spoke to me, I paid attention. The insistent voice kept reminding me to seek some help.

I was familiar with life coaching services through my work and had even used them to help with certain professional transitions. Somehow I knew this time would be different. This was a significant personal journey. The life I had been living no longer worked for me. I longed to feel satisfied with who I was. I wanted to enjoy my marriage again. I wanted to find a way to feel contented and happy. I wanted to focus on the future and not dwell on past issues. I had had several therapists over the years and was ready to take more ownership of my inner journey.

I wanted a life coach I trusted and felt safe with. I have found that having a coach in my life is a way I am led to access the answers that are residing within me. It is not someone telling me what to do but rather reflecting back to me what she sees in me and, in this way, I see what is possible. Several years prior, I had met Alison at a workshop. I was immediately drawn to her welcoming smile and warm energy and intrigued by her wise presence. When I heard she was accepting new clients, I knew I wanted her as my coach. My intuition told me that she would accept me just as I was and I would be open to her guidance.

I started meeting with her and we explored my inner life together. It became clear that I was ready to surrender, to give up the striving and pushing and try a new method. I was worried that resisting major life changes would seriously harm me. I had seen patients develop life-threatening diseases as a result of stress in their lives. I didn't want to be one of those statistics.

Over a series of sessions, I learned about the concept of "being versus doing." Most of my life had been focused on doing, with self-worth defined as action and accomplishment. What would it mean to focus on being?

It took many sessions with Alison, and lots of support and practice, before I learned that I am worthy of being loved for who I am and have nothing to prove to myself or others. It was contrary to much of what I had been taught as a young girl. I may have put aside the concept of a Higher Power I had to please and prove my self-worth to, but here I was, still judging myself based on my achievements. I grew aware of the seductive nature of proving worth through action, and I saw how I had been doing it without thinking. It was how I had always lived my life; I hadn't known any differently.

Thus began the work of shifting my perspective. The questions my coach encouraged me to ask were challenging and heart-opening. Could I accept the reality that my worth isn't tied to my accomplishments? It was a challenge to my lifelong beliefs, stemming from the young girl who wanted to belong. I opened my heart to the possibility of being

FINDING A NEW GUIDE

loved because of who I am rather than being loved for my capacity to help or work.

What if I could stop, breathe, and love myself for who I am, not for what I do? This was an obstacle for me. I struggled to love myself unconditionally, always harder on myself than on anyone else. I was challenged to reconsider the to-do list that kept me awake at night. Was it possible for me to be gentle with myself and accept who I was, even when I chose to rest while tasks were left undone? I worried that nothing would get done if I took this approach. I was still entrenched in my habits of striving and driving to prove myself. If I gave up my practice of trying so hard to complete my goals, I might end up being unproductive and lazy. I was proud of my strong work ethic and thought I might not be respected if I listened to Alison's suggestions and let certain projects slide. She was patient with me as we spent many sessions delving into these ideas.

Alison had further questions for me: If I focused on being, how might my health be impacted? What about my relationships? My emotional state? I longed for a lighthearted approach to life. I wanted to regain the fun and playfulness my husband and I used to feel in our marriage. I was willing to experiment if it might lead to feeling healthy and joyful again.

It was during this time that I was introduced to my Wise Woman. This was the image my coach had me visualize as she encouraged me to listen to my intuition. My Wise Woman was kind, loving, and radiant and accepted me just as I am. She welcomed me into her arms and held me gently as I confessed that I was lost and didn't know what would happen next.

I admitted I was afraid to trust her. What if she led me astray? Was it worth the risk? I was used to following the experts in my life, and I wasn't sure if she was one of them.

I heard her say I had wisdom deep within my soul that I could access anytime. I didn't need to ask experts what to do or follow the advice of those in authority. The pushing and striving were causing me physical and emotional problems. What did I have to lose? Why not give this new way of being a try?

My Wise Woman taught me about receiving joyously and how to expect abundance in my life. She encouraged me to take risks and trust that everything would work out. I rediscovered my zest for life as well as the importance of pleasure and play in creating a meaningful existence. She helped me see that I could embrace chaos and that uncertainty wasn't the scary monster I had thought it was.

We addressed my inner critic. I learned that facing my fear, rather than being a victim, was a way to take responsibility for my situation. It was an exhilarating new way of being. I was able to move ahead without being paralyzed by fear; I saw myself as capable and strong.

In one session with Alison, I heard my Wise Woman's voice clearly. Feeling her presence, I was inspired to follow her counsel. I saw the possibility of letting go of my strife and accepting my inherent worthiness without constantly worrying about what others expected of me. In the company of my coach and Wise Woman, all of this seemed possible.

Then I left and fell back into my old way of doing things. I wanted to make sure I was getting it right. I was worried I would upset others if I said what I wanted. What would they think if I said no to their requests? Would they reject me? Belonging was important to me, and

FINDING A NEW GUIDE

I was nervous I might lose friends if I acted differently. I caught myself looking to others for direction before I made a decision, just to be sure I was on the right track.

At times, I'd react to a situation, realizing only too late that I was giving in to my fear rather than paying attention to my inner wisdom. I wondered how to know if the voice I heard was my inner wisdom or my inner critic. I was so used to listening to external guides that it was challenging to differentiate these inner voices.

As I started really paying attention, I recognized that my inner critic's voice was rude and impatient, filling my mind with sweeping critical statements. "You never finish what you start. You're so messy. You're constantly abrasive when you speak up."

When I slowed down and took a deep breath, I heard the kind and inviting tones of my Wise Woman. She urged me to acknowledge what I wanted to do or say, encouraging me to trust myself. She reassured me that I was on the path to loving myself and this was the way for me to be open to receiving love from others in my life.

I became aware of how my body gave me clues as to which voice was speaking. When I noticed my fists were clenched and my shoulders were tense, it was my inner critic's voice that was loudest. When my Wise Woman was speaking, my body felt relaxed and open, my breathing deep and regular, and I didn't feel any tension in my body.

There were days when I thought, life was so much easier before I met my Wise Woman. I could just be myself. I didn't have to stop and think about which voice to listen to. This new path was taking so long to figure out. Once again, frustrated and impatient with myself, I felt awkward and wondered if I would ever feel at ease acting in this new way.

After years of practice, I've come to see my Wise Woman as a constant companion. I still have days when I forget about her presence, tempted to seek expert advice from outer sources. This usually happens when I have neglected to take time for myself. I do things out of a sense of duty or guilt. I compare myself to others and strive to do more in order to be as successful as they are. I go to a place of deficit and lose sight of the abundance in my life, measuring my self-worth by my accomplishments and feeling critical and judgmental. I slip back into the mess of pushing and striving to prove myself.

Once again, I remind myself that I have access to the wisdom within me simply by engaging my Wise Woman in conversation. I describe my dilemma to her and ask, "What would you say about this?" Each time, I am reassured by her presence as she guides me with love, encouragement, patience, and insight.

I can meet her anywhere: when I stop and listen to birdsong in the woods or breathe in the fresh air of a mountain trail; when I'm journalling or chopping vegetables for a pot of soup. I stop, take a deep breath, imagine her beside me, and there she is.

Sometimes she shows herself in a word to sink into when she communicates with me as I write in my journal, in the synchronicity of a line in a book, or in a phrase in a blog post that I know is a message from her. It could be a line that suggests I embrace the unknown in order to create adventure rather than giving in to fear.

Then there are the times when I'm not eager to follow her suggestions. I find myself resisting the idea that perhaps I am responsible for a certain coolness between my husband and me. She encourages me to get curious and talk to my husband to get his perspective. I feel her tenderly nudging me to look at what I may be responsible for as she suggests I take the initiative to clean up the mess. I am learning to trust that what she invites me to do is for the best.

While working with my coach, I continued working full time and came to love my career and the opportunities I had for professional advancement. After several decades as a nurse, I took on the role of consultant, facilitating workshops for healthcare leaders and supporting them in the areas of communication and leadership. This line of work suited me perfectly. I loved the interaction with workshop participants, and my years of healthcare experience gave me the confidence and credibility I needed. It was a wonderful vocation for me at this time of my working life.

Then, I came to an unexpected realization: I knew it was time to retire.

I could have worked several more years. I'd been working with an incredible team and loved teaching and coaching leaders. I was good at what I did. There seemed to be no real reason to quit.

Except for what my heart was telling me.

The position had been emotionally and physically demanding, and after seven years I had observed a shift in my energy and my outlook. There were times when I would push myself to be engaged with clients and colleagues. It was hard for me to say no when I was asked to do extra work. I was teaching self-care, a practice I found increasingly challenging to employ in my own life. I was fatigued, less joyful at work, and losing my zest for life.

So I took a stand for my health, in spite of any potential disappointment from my team. I was listening to my Wise Woman. She knew what was best for me.

The choice wasn't made lightly. I said yes to nurturing myself. Even though I knew there would be a drop in income, I went forward with retirement plans. My husband and I looked at our finances and decided to downsize. As I followed my inner wisdom, I saw how life was supporting my desires. We sold part of our home to our daughter and her husband and said yes to the adventure of sharing our family home with them. We settled into our newly built basement suite while they embarked on their life upstairs with their two sons.

Retiring from my full-time profession, I faced the uncertainty of my future. I found myself wondering where the trail was leading at this point in my life. It was overgrown and seemed to disappear up ahead. I struggled to get a sense of direction. Could I take it one step at a time and trust that I would find the way?

I knew I was beginning a new phase of life, and I took little steps on the path to trusting myself. I no longer had a boss to tell me what to do or give structure to my day. I asked myself what I wanted to do rather than following others' directions unthinkingly. Life took on a new rhythm. Where was this trail of retirement leading me?

I didn't resonate with the designation of being retired. I still had energy for doing what interested me and wanted to keep using my gifts. I just didn't want to stay in the organizational, institutional energy I had been working in all of my life. I made the assumption that being retired meant not having a goal to pursue or not being challenged to learn new things. I came to realize that this was actually a chance for me to discover what I could say yes to. Here was another opportunity for me to take control of my life and create my own experience.

As I looked back on my life, I saw times when I had made choices that brought meaning and joy to me—times when I changed jobs or sought out new challenges in my life, such as running marathons. These were examples of me following my inner wisdom even if I did not have the awareness of that yet.

With my newfound freedom, I read all kinds of books, listened to podcasts, and kept up with blog posts. I started following some coaches and writers who spoke the language I had been introduced to by Alison. They talked about their inner wisdom and about finding meaning in life by paying attention to what they desire. These thoughts continued to intrigue me. What might it look like to truly get in touch with what I want, and was doing so even possible? I found the ideas inspiring, especially as I experimented with slowing down and listening more deeply to myself, but I was still worried that such pursuits were selfish. Even after the work I had done and learning to listen to my Wise Woman, I caught myself thinking I was supposed to be considering others' needs before my own.

I joined a small group of women, a Sister Goddess Circle. We focused on pleasure and what that meant for women like us with children, grandchildren, jobs, and husbands. The ideas excited and surprised me. Did I even know what pleasure looked like for me? Did I know what I, Marjorie, really wanted? I was so used to thinking about my family or my friends' needs before mine that I hardly knew what I wanted for myself.

This question simmered in my soul. For several years, I continued to meet with the circle of women who witnessed me exploring the path of being versus doing, listening to my Wise Woman over the experts of my past, and figuring out what it was Marjorie wanted.

I was putting myself first and trusted that abundance was all around me.

EMERGING

»»———→

One day, I read a post by one of the most thoughtful, bright, humble writers I've ever read on feminine embodiment of love and possibility.

Tara Mohr was going to speak at a conference in Boulder, Colorado, and she invited her readers to check it out. I had been following Tara's blog posts for several months and was inspired by her commitment to encouraging women to use their voices boldly in both work and personal lives. She wrote about the inherent wisdom of women and how to access it.

Intrigued by the conference, I clicked on the link. Emerging Women Live was for women who were curious about living a life that would challenge them to become more of who they already are. It would be an opportunity for women to connect and celebrate, a chance for me to get to know myself better and find out what might be next for me. Moreover, it was in a part of the world I'd always wanted to visit. I envisioned the mountains, big sky, open fields, and lots of space. Plus, it was far from home—I could travel and get away. I was ready for that kind of adventure.

I'd been to plenty of conferences with colleagues and enjoyed the stimulation of listening to speakers and participating in small group discussions. But this was different: I was choosing to attend for no other reason than because I wanted to. My whole body was vibrating as I imagined taking part in the event. I was excited and nervous. It wasn't a work-related workshop. No one was paying for my registration. No one from my circle of friends would be there.

Could I justify that? Was I worthy of spending this amount of money on myself? Would it be worthwhile? I had a longing in my heart. I wondered if my Wise Woman had planted it there.

Intuitively, I knew I was meant to go.

With Alison's guidance, I had already been practicing paying attention to the sensations in my body. I could feel my stomach tighten when I was asked to do something I didn't want to do. Sometimes my face flushed or my hands clenched into fists before I even knew I had been triggered.

Faced with the prospect of this conference, my body was filled with energy and excitement. I couldn't stop thinking about going. I had butterflies every time I found myself imagining what it would be like to join such an inspiring event. I could already see myself in Boulder. I was slowly starting to understand the relationship between my body's sensations and their messages for me.

I was worried about talking to my husband about the costs involved, including registration, hotel costs, and flights. How could I find the money? We managed our finances as a partnership, and I wanted to be open with him about the trip expenses.

I talked to my coach and attained some clarity on how I wanted to show up in this courageous conversation. I was finally feeling I could trust myself to choose things that gave me joy. I was no longer listening to the voice that told me I should feel guilty about giving to myself. Thanks to our conversations and the Sister Goddess Circle, I'd been introduced to the concept of pleasure and following my desires. I was learning that when I am happy and fulfilled, the people around me benefit. When I have more to give, they are drawn to my joy and love of life.

This desire was big. As I breathed in the love I was learning to shower upon myself, I could see myself showing up with confidence and a deep knowing that, together, we could make this trip possible.

What followed was magical. As I described the conference and what it meant for me, my husband agreed that this was something for me to do. He heard my longing and sensed the significance of this for my life. We assessed our finances and realized it would be possible. Not only was I thrilled, but I was also filled with gratitude for his partnership and support of my dreams.

I felt excited and playful as I prepared to go. I studied the conference schedule and was inspired by the speakers and workshops. I booked my flights and made sure I had an extra day or two to explore the city. I chose to stay at the hotel where the conference was being held, not looking for cheap deals this time around. I wanted to be near the conference activities without worrying about finding my way around a new city. Along with the excitement, I detected a calm, grounded energy in my body. I wasn't preoccupied with worry over the trip details, and I felt confident as I prepared. I was following my heart, and all was well.

My Wise Woman was holding her hand out to me, understanding that I was in transition. I was in a place of in-between; no longer a full-time employee, I felt myself trying on a new identity, defining what "retired" could look like. In search of other ways to use my gifts, I wondered how I would contribute during the remaining years of my life. These were some of the questions I trusted would be answered at the conference.

I felt her telling me that this time would be a critical foundation for my next season; whatever was coming next would come out of this. I took the time to slow down and focus on being rather than pushing myself to do more and more. I recognized that preparing myself for the world that awaited me meant being intentional about pleasure and play. It meant taking the time to go on this trip, following my Wise Woman's invitation to take a leap. No waiting. No excuses. I would move forward before the whole path would appear, and I would trust that it would all become clear.

I packed my bags for the trip, carefully choosing items that were comfortable and beautiful. I had a funky pair of orange and yellow palazzo pants that I saw myself wearing to the dance party I was eager to attend. I felt like a goddess in them, and I wanted to bring that energy with me. I also packed a treasure chest of intentions for how I wanted to experience every step along the way.

In the workshops I facilitated for healthcare providers, I would talk with the participants about intentions, asking them to think about what they were bringing to the workshop in order to contribute to its success. I explained how that is different from an expectation, which is what we place on others. There might be an expectation of me to be a great facilitator or of the other participants to be wonderful learning partners. An intention is within our control—it's what we agree to do, say, or look for in order to create the best possible experience. I loved the power of setting an intention. It created a mindset that led me to find what I wanted in a situation.

I thought about what I could bring to the women's conference to enable a powerful experience. I had been experimenting with setting daily intentions, writing them in my journal each morning. I knew that doing so made a difference in how my day unfolded, and I was inspired to continue it for my trip. I was on a quest to find clues of abundance, wanting to find love and play in the smallest details. That's just what happened when I headed to the airport.

I enjoyed a delicious lunch with a glass of wine at the airport. I took pleasure in conversations with fellow travellers. The flight was filled with ease and fun. I was on an adventure. I couldn't stop smiling, and, of course, I received smiles in return.

I couldn't remember the last time I'd travelled by myself. Vacations had always been with my husband, children, or other women. It became evident to me how often I had thought of others' needs before my own, so often making choices based on what was best for my kids or my husband. Now it was just me; I was the only one to consider. I had to be clear about what I wanted.

It was a new experience, and I was deliberate in choosing what was best for me in each moment. I bought the magazines that appealed to me and spent the whole flight as I wished, journalling, reading, dozing off, imagining what adventures lie ahead…. I soon came to love the independence of solo travel.

I checked into the hotel, feeling luxury surround me. My room had big windows looking out onto the mountains. I smiled when I saw the soaker tub surrounded by fluffy towels and candles. I took a deep breath of satisfaction as I wrapped myself in the robe provided for me and crawled under the cozy blankets. I was here!

I booked a massage simply because I wanted to. I ordered room service and continued to enjoy the sumptuousness of my surroundings. I was beginning to see myself as a woman worthy of being pampered and treated royally.

I had arrived in Boulder early and decided to make the most of my time alone in a new place. With directions from the hotel concierge, I explored the city, enjoying the quaint restaurants and beautiful shops. I felt a sense of adventure and found myself reaching out to strangers easily. I complimented a woman's gorgeous dress over lunch, and she told me where she'd bought it. Off I went, catching a bus to the shop, where I wasn't surprised to find a dress I loved. I told the saleswoman why I was visiting Boulder, and we shared a moment of connection, talking about the importance of women following their desires. I bought the dress and a coat sweater to go with it.

These clothes represented "the new me." I was worthy of having beautiful things, and I felt joy and gratitude as I took them back to the hotel. I was putting myself first and trusted that abundance was all around me. Abundance showed up in the connection with the saleswoman and in the kindness of the woman I met at lunch. I had set the intention to find love and play everywhere, so I recognized the significance of these people appearing in my life. I was in the flow of receiving. I was able to buy these clothes with freedom and gratitude and knew I would feel confident and feminine in them.

Then the conference started. In a buzz of excited conversation, we got our name tags and conference packages. Entering the hotel ballroom, I was surprised by what I saw. It was nothing like the professional conferences I had attended in the past—instead of a sterile, business-like atmosphere, there was lively music playing. The stage was overflowing with beauty: a big pink couch was surrounded by lamps, soft grey carpet, and an extravagant display of brightly coloured flowers.

With over 300 women registered, I wondered how I would ever find my way with such an overwhelming crowd. I suddenly felt shy and awkward. What was I doing at a place like this? I felt my confidence slip away like fog dissipates unnoticed on a sunny morning.

A smiling volunteer welcomed me and invited me to join a circle of eight women. Feeling nervous for the first time in nearly twenty-four hours, I wondered which group would be the one for me? I walked to a circle near the front of the room and sat down in an empty chair. I didn't know any of these women, but, instead of falling into old patterns of fear of not belonging, I recalled my intention to find love and play everywhere, and the butterflies in my stomach settled down. There was a feeling of intimacy as we sat in chairs with no tables separating us.

I smiled at the woman sitting next to me whose name tag read "Sylvia." She told me that she'd come from San Francisco, and, like me, she was there on her own. I felt an immediate kinship with her. She was young and vivacious with an intriguing twinkle in her eye. I thought she would be fun to spend time with and wondered if she'd feel the same way about me. I took a deep breath and waited to meet the others, feeling relieved to have this personal time with a small group at the start of the conference.

All of the women in the circle were open and vulnerable as we answered the questions posed by the woman leading us from the stage. The questions challenged us and helped us dig deep into our newly-forming relationships. There was a shared commitment to being fully present and taking personal responsibility for making this conference meaningful. We were a diverse range of ages and backgrounds, but our desire to learn about feminine leadership was a thread joining our hearts together.

We met daily, sharing meals and getting to know each other more intimately as we talked and laughed. The thrill of being part of a circle of women reminded me of my Sister Goddess Circle back home. I was accepted and loved, delighted to be part of such a heart-opening experience.

Sylvia and I spent hours together. We sat beside each other at the main sessions and checked in after our individual workshops. We both loved being outside and went for long walks, talking and laughing. I hadn't expected to meet a good friend, but I did. It was an unexpected gift, the icing on the cake after all the amazing speakers and workshops.

While there were many wonderful speakers and inspirational speeches, it wasn't the content of the conference but who I became as a result of it that was most significant. It was a place where I could trust myself to choose things that filled me with joy. I was letting go of the voice that would tell me I should feel guilty about giving to myself. My heart was blown wide open. I was filled with creativity and love for myself—and everything around me. I became more of who I am meant to be.

My trip to Boulder was about me being a vessel to receive. Having spent most of my life as a helper and focusing on how I could give to others, I was ready to allow others to give to me. I saw how it was possible to receive from others in a natural and gracious way when I was filled with love for myself. The paradox of receiving is that I must first give to myself, a practice which began with this trip.

My sense of commitment to myself as an authentic woman comes from within. It comes when I act not for the sake of pleasing others but when my outer actions match my inner values. When I am in touch with my emotions without fear of letting them show. When I speak up to others without fear of sharing my opinion, even if they disagree. As I allow myself pleasure, I feel calm, happy, rested, and energized. From this place within, all of life flows.

There were people there who were meant to meet me. There were those whom I was meant to meet. I went with the intention of being open and receiving from a place of being. I had nothing to prove as I waited to see who would come along to join me. I saw that I never have to apologize for who I am. Instead, I marvelled, Isn't the world lucky I'm here! The participants wanted my wisdom. I had gifts to offer. I was authentic as I met women from all over the world. I experienced the thrill of meeting like-minded women, no matter their profession, age, or financial status. We laughed and shared our stories with love, connecting with ease and joy.

When I showed up in my strong feminine power, I was an example to the women I met. I owned my "eldership." I didn't apologize for my age, instead celebrating my life experiences and sharing my wisdom when it was requested. My career changes, adjustment to retirement, long-term marriage, and grandchildren were aspects of life the women were curious about navigating. I asked questions to get them thinking about their situation differently, reframing a problem or encouraging their curiosity rather than being judgmental about a conflict or tense situation.

I gave new meaning to the word "strong." I learned that I'm only weak when I pretend to be someone I'm not, when I don't listen to myself and act against my desires. Being strong means seeing myself in the most favourable light I can imagine. That's when I'm following my inner Wise Woman's voice. From this powerful place, I say yes to life.

I returned home from my trip and saw that it was now "being time" in a specific and intentional way. It was time for me to receive love and support at home. This meant being vulnerable and humble. Choosing carefully and with discernment those with whom I would be real and share myself.

I am not alone. I belong. I have a place here. I am loved. I am LOVE.

As the months went by, I discovered a yearning in my heart to share with other women what I had experienced at the Emerging Women Conference. I knew I wanted support in order to do this, so I enrolled in a life coaching program. After a year, I became a coach myself, working with individual clients and hosting women's circles.

The vision of hosting a day-long retreat for women came to me one day. I loved the retreats I attended during my coaching program. They were a time of play, reflection, and deep connection with other women, plus they involved yummy food, a beautiful setting, and a sense of sisterhood that warmed my heart.

As a result of these retreats, I saw myself differently. I was part of an intimate circle of soul sisters where I felt accepted and loved. We laughed and cried and witnessed each other. I was more aware of my abilities as a coach and was able to gently accept areas where I wanted to expand and grow. The energy of celebration and support was something I wanted to have women experience at the retreat I was planning.

Was that possible?

I had been talking about my desire for months. Now, the details were coming together, and it was time to make it happen!

I sent out the invitations, eagerly awaiting the responses. Over the past year, many women had indicated they were interested, and I was excited for them to have the chance to come and play with me.

I waited. I waited some more. It didn't go as I expected. I got some replies: "No" or "Not now." Some included reasons why they wouldn't be able to come; others didn't give a reason at all. Some didn't even reply.

I was angry and deeply disappointed. I had set the intention that I would have a group of six to eight women join me. Now it looked like maybe only one or two would attend. Viewing myself as a failure, I cried as I wrote in my journal. I started to doubt myself in a variety of ways. I questioned my ability to communicate to women the benefits of attending a retreat. I worried whether my plans for the day were not inviting and fun enough for women to say yes to. Maybe I was wrong in thinking I could host a retreat. I convinced myself that I must not be cut out to host retreats. I was jealous of all the other retreat leaders with dozens of participants and felt insecure in my role as a coach. I lost my joy in planning the day-long program. What was the point? It may not even be happening.

I was grumpy and irritable, and my body was tense. I didn't want to tell anyone what was happening. I withdrew and kept to myself. I wanted to cancel the retreat, even though there were still several weeks to go.

It was during this time I had a regularly scheduled session with my coach, Alison. It gave me a safe place to share what was happening. I expressed my anger, and she listened, encouraging me to fully feel my emotions. All of them—the raw pain, jealousy, anxiety, insecurity, anger.... Could

I allow myself to feel this messy mix of perfectly valid emotions and love myself in the midst of it all? Without shame, apology, or pretense?

It wasn't easy for me, but I gave myself permission to feel deeply and allowed the tears to flow. I trusted I would be okay. I sat with my emotions and noticed my energy shift. My breathing slowed, and I felt stillness and peace in my body. The intensity had eased. It was as if I could observe myself from above. I saw a glimmer of light in my darkness.

Alison softly asked, "What do you think is under your anger?" She explained that disappointment happens when we are filled with judgment about something. I knew I had been judging the women who had said no and struggled with my reply. Didn't they know what they were missing? Did they not value their personal development? Where were their priorities?

She wondered what my Wise Woman might be feeling. I closed my eyes and took a deep breath. I saw that she was sad for these women, rather than judgmental. It was then that I found my sadness for the women who wouldn't be joining me. I also found sadness for myself—a cleaner, softer emotion than the anger and judgment I'd earlier expressed. I was no longer shaming myself for being upset; instead, I was feeling love and self-compassion.

I chose to focus on my sadness rather than my anger. I trusted the women had valid reasons and were making the best choice for themselves. I released my expectations as to how many would say yes and continued planning the retreat with renewed intention, energy, and creativity.

As it turned out, two women attended. We had a rich time of connection, play, and learning. We explored the nearby beach and forest. We coloured and shared stories and photos of ourselves as little girls. Lunch was at my favourite heritage hotel, The Sylvia. Only being three of us, it was possible to eat out. There was a sense of intimacy that may not have been attainable with a larger group. The success of a retreat isn't in the numbers, a lesson I learned that day.

I now see myself differently. I am a woman who holds retreats. I can say yes to the challenge of hosting one without the certainty of where the path might lead me, and I can hear women say no to it without feeling angry or like a failure. I may still feel sad, and that's okay. No longer numbing or shoving the feelings down, I remind myself that allowing myself to feel deeply is how I move through to the other side.

I can choose to be a student of my experience and investigate the process. I am an observer of my own emotional journey, and, as a result, I'm able to do the work of self-acceptance. I lean into the practice of trusting myself and not allowing my inner critic to stop me in my tracks. Along the way, I see the benefit of receiving from others and finding abundance in unexpected places. Just as planning a retreat was a leap into the unknown, I know there is more to learn about taking risks and being responsible for my life and the actions I take. It is as I do this that I am able to lead, hold, and be a guide for other women who want to do the same for themselves.

Saying yes to life requires me to have the courage to lace up my hiking boots and trek along the trail, no matter how steep or rugged it is. As I keep going, I explore what it looks like to trust more deeply, face uncertainty more fearlessly, live more authentically, and be a true leader more confidently. As I navigate these paths with curiosity, I am struck by the richness of what is revealed to me. I enjoy the amazing views, the company of fellow hikers, and the sense of purpose and peace that fills my heart.

TRUST

Taking the Trail of Trust

What do I mean by "trust"? And what does it look like?

The Merriam-Webster dictionary defines trust as "reliance on the integrity, strength, and ability of a person or thing." To trust is to have a confident expectation of something or a person on which one relies.

There are numerous areas of life in which I practice trust. These range from having trust in a Higher Power to trusting that the hot water will be there for my morning shower to trusting that I will be safe as I drive my car on the freeway. I trust that money will show up when needed and that there are people willing to encourage me with my life dreams.

As I explore the trail of trust, I investigate another perspective on trust. What does it look like to trust myself? Is that even possible? How do I know I am trustworthy? What if I make a mistake when I follow my own advice?

Given I spent most of my life following the guidance of those with authority over me—whether those were teachers in school, the church's teachings, or my boss—I did not know how to listen to my inner wisdom. As I was growing up, I was not encouraged to question the experts, and since I was the type of person who wanted to please others, I rarely argued or disagreed with anyone I saw as my superior.

Once I discovered that I had access to wisdom within myself, I had a lot of learning to do—or rather *unlearning*. In the process, I have come to rely on and have confidence in my Wise Woman, my intuition. This is a trail I continue to travel and new vistas regularly appear. The journey of trusting myself is winding, uphill, and full of surprises—and one I would not have wanted to miss.

Make Friends With My Inner Critic

We all live with an inner critic. It's a part of us we must learn to embrace and listen to in order to know what it needs. It may even have something to offer us. We shouldn't necessarily take its advice—most of the time its perspective is skewed and biased because its main priority is to keep us safe. The more we venture out of the safety of our current existence and into living the life we're meant to live, the louder the inner critic gets.

For the first few months of writing my book, I made really good progress: the Table of Contents came together with a flow that covers the themes of the book, and I completed the chapter outlines with ease. My editor then suggested I shift my focus to the contents of each chapter, moving away from structure and format. I knew it was time to do this.

The problem was, I was stuck.

The words didn't come to me. I felt no energy to write. I checked my phone, scrolled through social media, read a novel, took a long nap. I snacked on junk food and even did housework to distract myself.

Meanwhile, a certain voice in my head got louder and louder. My "inner mean girl" is a bit of a bully. She would ask, "Who do you think you are writing a book? You're going to make a fool of yourself. You'll never have the energy or stamina to keep going. This project is too ambitious for you. Who would want to read about your ideas, anyway?"

As she echoed her refrain, I experienced a mess of emotions and thoughts. I felt inadequate and incapable of being an author. I was fearful and anxious. My stomach was upset. I was irritable and impatient, and I disliked myself. I wanted to crawl into a cave for the remainder of the year. Maybe no one will even remember I'm writing a book.

Rather than sit at my laptop and pretend to write while she badgered on, I decided to move my body and walk around my neighbourhood. I breathed deeply and wondered if there's a way through this messy time. As I walked, my mind floated back to a coaching session several years prior. Delving into the concept of my inner critic, my coach led me through a visualization process. I recalled our technique of relating to my inner mean girl.

Home from my walk, I imagined my critic sitting beside me speaking loudly. I remained quiet as she chattered away—she's afraid that writing means I'm wasting money, not being truly productive, and no fun to be with. What kind of summer will my husband and I enjoy if I'm stuck sitting at my laptop all the time? She's afraid that my friends will be critical if I say no to time with them, that my family will be critical of my obsession with the project, that they'll see me as selfish and uncaring. She told me that even if I do write the book, I'll be disappointed with it.

I tried talking to her, and she just got louder.

Then I knelt in front of her and put my hands on her knees. I looked into her eyes and asked her what she's afraid of. She kept chattering. I remained silent and waited. Her voice changed. Softly she said, "Be careful. Don't take on too many risks…." For the first time, I saw the worry and concern in her eyes and knew how much she cares for me.

Another voice joined the conversation. My soul's inner wisdom, helping me tell my critic what I now know. "I'm going to be okay. I have help. I'm not doing this alone. I want a challenge. I feel excited and nervous at the same time. I'd feel really sad if I couldn't do this. I will get the support I need."

"What do you need to come along with me?" I asked. "Don't ignore me completely," she warned. "Don't be foolish. Don't wear yourself out and get sick. Sometimes there's some truth to be found in my worry for you. I want to keep you safe. Give me credit for my intent."

I was committed to turning toward her to look into her eyes. She wanted to be seen, and when she is seen she becomes quiet. I stepped into a relationship with her, welcoming her home. I had the strength to face my critic. It felt miraculous to me, thinking back to the many times I angrily pushed her away and yelled at her to be quiet. I was often frustrated by her nagging and would distract myself in order to drown out her voice. But doing so prevented me from being creative and enjoying my life. When I numbed the feelings of inadequacy and shame, I also numbed any possible emotions of joy or loving peace. When I can face her directly, I am deeply touched, recognizing how far I've come.

Now, I'm able to hold her as well as all those aspects of myself I had been keeping in exile.

Acknowledging my inner critic's presence led me to open up a deeper knowing of the inner wisdom that speaks to my heart. My coaching sessions with Alison would often focus on how to relate to my inner critic. As we explored this, Alison would prompt me to slow down and listen carefully. Could I hear any other voices? I noticed the sweet sound of a voice telling me I was loved. I came to recognize that this was my inner wisdom, and I can trust her.

There are different words to describe this voice. It can be called intuition, sixth sense, a "soul's guide" or, as I say, a "Wise Woman."

As I have the awareness to look into the eyes of my inner critic and listen to what it wants from me, I see my situation in a new light. Shutting out the voice of criticism doesn't work. Distractions and numbing are only short-term solutions. I choose to take the courageous step of slowing down, hearing what my inner critic is trying to say, and trusting it is safe to move forward.

Receive With Joy

I ran home with the exciting news. Our grade five class was going on a bus trip to Regina. We would see the legislative buildings and the RCMP Musical Ride. I would be visiting a city I had never seen, and it would be an adventure with my friends. I could hardly wait.

Then I got the news that we couldn't afford the $5 fee. I was heartbroken and disappointed. Life wasn't fair.

A few days later, my parents called me over to them after supper to tell me I could go after all. A family in the church had heard about the situation and offered to cover the cost. I was at once grateful and happy, but also embarrassed that I had to depend on others to give me the money to do what I wanted.

Learning to receive has been a challenge for me over the years. It doesn't come naturally. It requires me to translate from my "original language" of pleasing, which so often says no to me. The practice of receiving, on the other hand, is linked to my choice to say yes. It's a path to trusting myself and hearing the voice of my Wise Woman.

When I receive, I admit I cannot do it alone, which is vulnerable and humbling to do. I initially struggled with pride, wishing to come across as strong and capable. Over time, I realized that receiving help is a sign of strength.

Before I retired, I was in the midst of facilitating a two-day workshop with a colleague. On the second day, I awoke with a scratchy throat and hoarse voice. I couldn't speak above a whisper. Feeling healthy otherwise, I chose to stay on but with a less active role. My co-facilitator took the lead in presenting the material, and I had the chance to be a recipient and listen. It turned out to be a powerful learning experience that transformed my view of receiving. The class witnessed our example of partnership and quiet leadership, and I found some healing as well as a deep connection with others because I could sit back and receive without apology. Rather than seeing myself as a failure, I started to link the act of receiving to the practice of trusting myself. When I receive, I am putting myself first and noticing what it is I want.

I've spent most of my life accessing my masculine energy and pushing through at all costs. It was an integral part of my role as the primary wage earner of our family. This masculine energy kept me organized and drove me to succeed and overcome obstacles. These are positive attributes that served me well. I am proud of my accomplishments over the years. However, I seldom stopped to check in with myself and see what it was I wanted. Even as a young girl, I remember working hard, often taking menial jobs like babysitting disobedient toddlers and cleaning houses. I really didn't enjoy them, but it was up to me to earn money, so I would never again need to rely on others. I wouldn't be a charity case. It wasn't easy to see myself as worthy of receiving.

When I was fourteen years old, my friend Gisela and I had planned an adventure for the day and were taking the bus downtown to go shopping. As we were leaving, her father called us over and gave us each twenty dollars for spending money. I couldn't believe it! What a treat to have money to spend on myself. Even though I worked hard to get the money I earned, I had trouble valuing it. The idea that money was available for my pleasure and joy was a foreign concept. I took it for granted and didn't appreciate what I could do with it, an attitude that carried on into my adult years. I saw money as the enemy. As long as I saw money as a means to an end, there never seemed to be enough.

This money story has had an impact on me over the years. It was only recently that I heard about a different way of viewing money which was more empowering. Instead of seeing money as something I devalued or felt shame around, I could see it as an energy exchange that flows between individuals. The power I had assigned it in the past wasn't the path to a joyful life.

My husband and I love spending time in Vancouver. A few years ago, we wanted to rent a small place near the ocean that would be a place of retreat for us. The dream seemed audacious and unrealistic when we began looking, but we knew in our hearts we wouldn't give up on our quest.

We looked and looked and nothing seemed right. One was too dark. Another was too far away from the water. Others were too expensive. We kept looking and waiting for the right one.

The experience of finding our city home, the Beach Towers apartment, was an example of the power of being open to possibility as I surrendered to the flow of receiving in my life. The result was better than I would ever have imagined!

After all our searching and waiting, we got a call saying a place had just become available to view. It just so happened that Alison and I were having lunch nearby that day. Together we went to look. It was a one-bedroom suite on the nineteenth floor with an unobstructed view of the ocean. The rent was within our budget. It was steps away from the sea wall and the forest trails.

I was overcome with excitement and joy. I looked at Alison, and she smiled. "Of course you would find this place!" We both felt my Wise Woman's presence with us. What a beautiful synchronicity to have my coach by my side as I stepped into this apartment suite. After all, it was because of my coaching with Alison that I knew I could trust my inner wisdom.

I felt a wave of joy and realization that everything had been waiting for me. Ever since my husband and I decided to find a second home in the city, I had a clear picture in my mind of what I wanted in the apartment:

a view, lots of light, and close proximity to Stanley Park. I trusted that a place like this would show up. When I found our place, all I needed to do was receive it with gratitude and a sense of being blessed.

I still feel shivers as I reflect on that experience with my friend Gisela. I wasn't given the money because I needed it. Both of us were given something from her father's generous heart, and, as a result, I received with joy. I was unable to put this into words at the time, but I now understand it was one of the first times in my life when I felt worthy of receiving a gift.

The key for me is to receive fully the love that is all around me. I want to feel worthy of being blessed and not diminish the richness of the gift. I feel humbled and excited when I accept the fact that everything is waiting for me to say yes to it.

Why have I chosen to learn this new way of being? Why not embrace my role as a "doer" and leave the receiving to others?

As I receive, my energy is expansive, generous, light, and happy. I'm aware of a sovereign energy within me. I am blessed. I am a blessing. When I live my life with this energy flowing through me, I show up authentically. I accept who I am and put myself first. Because of this, everyone around me benefits.

So, I stop, take a breath, and choose to speak the language of receiving. In so doing, I experience a new energy force. Feminine energy flows through me. This energy is open to what is offered, sensing from the soul when to take action and receiving in a variety of forms. I say yes to a cup of coffee offered me by a friend (or stranger!). I respond to compliments with a simple thank-you. I ask for what I need without apology. I trust that I am worthy of receiving these gifts and speaking up for myself in this way.

What a beautiful affirmation of the truth I am learning. The Universe will provide, often in surprising ways. I'm struck by the power of finding miracles every day. I'm able to experience abundance countless times. There's an infinite supply of it, and, receiving with open arms and a soft heart, I create the possibility and openness for more. I now see myself differently, as a woman with trust and courage. I joyously receive the abundance and step forward on a difficult and winding path without knowing the destination. As I move forward, the path appears and I am provided for.

Expect Abundance

I left my hotel and walked down the street, taking in the bustling energy of it all—the shops and smells and sounds. I was in New York City, and I was on a mission. I was going to find a piece of jewellery.

Not just any piece, but something that would be a symbol for me as I attended the following day's coaching retreat. I was in the midst of a year-long coaching program, and the retreat was an opportunity to meet my coaching colleagues in person. We had been meeting virtually for the past six months as we held sister circles and one-on-one coaching sessions. I loved the partnerships that developed as a result, and I felt accepted by the young women I was studying with. I was old enough to be their mother, but rather than feeling out of place, I embraced the opportunity to connect with their vibrant, youthful energy.

When I joined this coaching program, I immediately had the feeling of "coming home." I met like-minded women who were eager to share from their hearts and listen deeply to my soul's longings. We grew to trust each other and spent many hours practicing our coaching skills with each other. It was much more than a theoretical course to gain a coaching certificate. We accepted each other with love and learned new ways of being. There was abundance in the variety of ages, ethnic groups, and life experiences. They respected me for mine and considered me a wise woman.

One young woman told me that she was inspired by my taking a course like this at this time of my life. She didn't know any other women that would do what I was doing, and she wanted me to know how much this meant to her. I had tears of joy in my eyes as we embraced and I received her gift to me. Another woman was newly married and curious about what kept my marriage vibrant after being with my husband for over forty years. This was a humbling experience as I reflected on the key components of my marriage with her. I became aware of just how much I had in my life because of the love that Al and I have nurtured over the years. I found myself honouring my age and my life experience. I focused on the abundance of my life rather than feeling insecure and inadequate in the presence of all these talented and beautiful young women. To this day, I value this experience of sisterhood that places an emphasis on collaboration and cooperation as women without judgment, competition, or comparison.

As I anticipated meeting the women in person, I wanted to remember that I was Queen Marjorie, open to giving and receiving with an open heart. On my walk, I thought to myself, what symbol would I find?

A consignment store's artistic window displays caught my attention. Excited, I opened the door and looked around. The clothing, shoes, and jewellery were a feast for the senses. I looked at rings, necklaces, and brooches. Then I saw a bracelet with soft grey-lavender stones that turned out to be freshwater pearls. I was in love. It was more than I wanted to spend, but I trusted I was being provided for and worthy of such an investment. I needed help putting the bracelet on my wrist and smiled, catching the significance of this. Each time I wore this bracelet, I would need to ask for help and then receive.

Over the next few years, I practiced seeing myself as worthy of investment. I travelled to conferences across the country. I enrolled in a coaching master class. I hired a virtual assistant. I bought a website and hired a designer to support me in creating my business site. I moved ahead, trusting that money would show up, and it did. When I needed funds for the coaching program, my retirement organization asked me to lead workshops for healthcare managers. I declared myself a life coach and awaited clients. It didn't take long—people had heard about me from their colleagues and contacts. They called, wanting to work with me as their coach. Many of them told me they were inspired by my story of investing in myself and expecting abundance. I saw myself as a partner with money. It was no longer the enemy. When it appeared, I replied, "Of course!"

Abundance shows up in many ways other than in the form of money: the support and encouragement for my book from my family and close friends; the friend who buys me lunch; the gift of staying in a luxurious home for a weekend getaway; or the gift of synchronicity, two seemingly unrelated events that assure me everything is going according to a master plan.

I'll meet a woman at a coffee shop who asks me to coach her. I'll come across a certain blog post and feel called to attend a specific retreat. I'll learn of a book and hear people talking about how much they've learned from it in the following days. When I read it, my life is enriched and transformed. I experience the abundance of paying attention to my inner wisdom and see evidence of being led as I practice listening to my soul's deep whisper.

As I walked back to my hotel, the bracelet glowed on my wrist. I felt happy and light-hearted. I greeted the gentleman at the front desk and showed him my recent purchase. He looked at me and said, "You know the name Marjorie means pearl, right? It was my wife's name too."

I was moved and touched by this coincidence knowing full well in my heart that it wasn't really a coincidence at all. It was yet another example of synchronicity. We both smiled and agreed that the bracelet was perfect for me. The bracelet itself was a symbol of the practice I wanted to remember: the importance of receiving abundance graciously.

I'm no longer surprised when things just "happen" to occur. Instead, I smile and say "of course." In the past, events like these went unnoticed without my awareness of their significance. Now, I pay attention to my inner wisdom and open my eyes to what happens. Such events are evidence that I'm on the right track. In those moments, I'm filled with gratitude and a sense of deep knowing that all is well.

The more I trust and take risks, the more I experience the gifts that are available for me. Every day, I'm on the lookout for more abundance in my life that I know I'm worthy of receiving.

Take Risks

It was a hot summer day in 1994 and our family was on vacation in Winnipeg. We decided to go to a movie downtown to escape the heat. But first, I needed a payphone. I had a call to make. I was nervous and excited and couldn't wait any longer to hear the news.

I had applied for a job as a public health nurse back home in British Columbia, and the manager had told me to call her on this specific day to find out if the job was mine. The months leading up to this exciting event were filled with periods of questioning and doubt. I wrestled with the risk of making a change in my job.

I had come to recognize that my job as head nurse in the recovery room wasn't for me. It may have looked as if I had the perfect career—I'd worked there for many years and had great benefits, six weeks of vacation time, and a top salary. I had received recognition for my work and was well-respected as a leader.

Why would I want to leave such a job? Why was I feeling dissatisfied?

Over time I saw that my internal values were incongruous to the values I was expected to uphold at work. I knew I wanted a life in which my work was only part of my focus. I wanted to enjoy time off, not to be constantly at the mercy of my work schedule. I desired an environment that supported my health and happiness, and I sensed that was no longer the case at work. The ever-increasing workload, overtime, and unrealistic expectations placed on us had become the norm. It didn't matter if we had other plans or were exhausted.

I found myself caught between doctors' demands and staff needs. It seemed I couldn't please anyone. When I tried speaking up for myself and the nurses, I was insulted and disrespected by the doctors and other leaders. My job no longer gave me respect or a voice for my values. I began to consider finding a new job.

It was around then that I heard about the job in public health nursing. I was intrigued but afraid of what saying yes to the position might mean.

I would risk losing my job security. The new role was only available for a year while a nurse was on maternity leave. If she came back to work, I'd be without a job. The public health organization was a separate union from my hospital job, which meant a drop in my pay scale and loss of seniority. No more long stretches of vacation time or generous benefits. And on top of that, the job required a car, another seemingly overwhelming expense.

There was also the risk of needing to learn new skills. I'd never worked as a public health nurse and wondered if I'd fit in to this type of career. What if I didn't like it? Was I being foolish in leaving my hospital job for the unknown?

Then I thought about what might happen if I didn't make a change. There was a negative impact on my health and happiness that I could only envision getting ever more burdensome. The thought of staying in that environment indefinitely was unthinkable. It was time for something new.

My heart was pounding and my hands were sweaty as I dropped my coins into the payphone. I had butterflies in my stomach and my legs felt like jelly. The uncertainty was taking over my mind and body. I wanted this job with all my heart and soul.

The phone rang and rang. Finally, the manager answered. I took a deep breath and asked about my application status. There was a long pause before she told me, "Marjorie, I'd be delighted if you accepted this job." I could hear the smile in her voice. "I really enjoyed our conversation. You're definitely qualified, and I think you'd fit the team well. When can you start?"

My mind was a whirl. I could hardly believe what I heard. I told her I would send in my resignation to the hospital that very day. I wanted to start as soon as possible. She congratulated me and was looking forward to welcoming me as part of the Public Health Nursing Group.

I was flying high! Hanging up the phone, I ran back to my family. With a big smile, I told them the news. My heart was singing, and I felt a deep knowing that this was exactly what I was meant to do next in my career.

I had applied for the new job even though the path ahead was full of unknown twists and turns. It was a powerful and emboldening experience, one of the first major steps I took in life without knowing what lay ahead. That particular job did last only one year. Little did I know, there would be increased funding in public health, allowing me to secure a permanent position when a new job opened up "just in time."

I felt encouraged to notice how risk-taking can pay off. Taking a risk wasn't as risky as it had seemed. I look back at this experience as a key example of how I started trusting myself regarding what's best for me and taking responsibility for my life. There would have been an even greater risk to my health and happiness had I not left my position as head nurse in the hospital. Changing jobs was worth it for me.

When I take a chance, I let go of controlling what happens next. This means I must trust I am able to handle the outcome, whatever it may be. I take full responsibility for how I face the events of the future, focusing on what I have control over and releasing the rest.

Choose Responsibility

Some of the biggest risks I've taken are in the arena of personal relationships. I used to think I was overly sensitive and shouldn't let little things bother me, wary of being viewed as someone who can't let things go. Why make a big deal of a little issue or misunderstanding? I should just get on with life.

I've come to realize that it's better for me to face what bothers me rather than ignore it and hope it'll go away. When I push issues aside and pretend they never happened, nothing is fixed. In fact, even little things often resurface in larger form.

A dear coaching colleague and I meet for regular calls and keep in touch in between to share our deepest fears and frustrations. I've come to count on her support as a place of safety that witnesses and cares for me. She responds to my pain with words of wisdom and accepts me just as I am.

When I was at my wits' end about how to help my husband's parents adapt to their assisted living situation, I sent a long, stormy message to my friend about my anger and my sense of helplessness. I counted on her reply, waited, and got nothing. I was surprised and hurt by her lack of response. Did she not care about me after all? Why would she ignore my cry for help?

I knew we had a call coming up. What was I going to do? Stuff down my hurt feelings and pretend all was well? I wrote in my journal and saw my pattern of wanting to ignore upsets like this, tending to go to a place of self-shame for being so sensitive and easily hurt.

Then I caught myself. I stopped and breathed deeply. I imagined my Wise Woman sitting with me and listened to her sweet whisper. I knew I was being called to check in with my friend, and share my experience of pain and hurt. I had butterflies in my tummy. I wanted to cancel the call. I didn't know how I would be received. What if I hurt her feelings? What if she didn't want to continue our relationship after I told her how I felt?

I made a choice. I trusted myself to be able to share from a place of love and authenticity, and I trusted her to accept me. The risk was worth it because I valued our relationship and our clear, open connection.

What happened next was above and beyond what I could have dreamed possible.

When my phone rang and I saw it was her, I took a deep breath and answered her call. I told her I wanted to check something out with her before getting into our conversation, telling her about my disappointment and what I wanted from her. I cried as I shared my longing to be heard and seen by her. I asked her if she could tell me why she didn't respond to my message.

She graciously listened, waiting quietly until I was done. She was shocked she hadn't replied: she said she'd been thinking about me daily. She was sure she had responded and apologized for not ensuring her message was sent. She acknowledged my pain and told me how much she cared for me. She thanked me for my courage to tell her what I felt and was struck by the power of my transparency and authenticity. In fact, she wanted our relationship to include even more of it.

I felt a lightness and deep sense of peace as we continued our conversation. I shared myself and she, herself. We engaged in the gift exchange of love and care for one another. By disclosing my hurt and pain, our relationship became closer.

An important aspect of taking responsibility for myself is checking in with others about what's really going on for them rather than making up a story and acting on my own assumptions. When I do check out my story, I'm often surprised to find the issue may have nothing to do with me or there's a reasonable explanation that leads to a productive change in our relationship. It's all too easy to blame others for problems based on my perception of things. Only when I'm curious and responsible for myself can there be clarity and healthy interaction.

It doesn't always result in getting the kind of response I want. Sometimes when I ask for clarification from people or tell them about my hurt or sadness, instead of offering me compassion, they may get defensive and argue that I'm the problem. When this happens, I feel sad and wish it would turn out differently. I don't enjoy the messiness of a broken relationship. I'm also reminded that while I'm responsible for how I show up and respond, I'm not responsible for how others react. As I trust myself, I learn to focus on what I have control over and let go of the rest.

People long to be seen, witnessed, heard, accepted, and loved. This looks different for everyone, and we can take responsibility to check in with others to learn how they'd like to be treated. Equally, if I want to be seen, how do I take responsibility for my experience and ask for that?

Love is open-handed and non-judgmental. This means I have the courage to say what I want and am willing to accept that I may not get what I ask for. I accept the other person's response and release the idea that I'm unworthy or unloved if they don't give me what I desire.

There's usually a story behind each person's behaviour. I don't know their whole experience, and I may never know. Am I able to assume their best intentions? Can I choose to extend grace and see them as desiring love from me?

Life is a series of relationship adventures. Some are magical. Others are messy. A single relationship often contains both aspects. Taking responsibility for myself and owning my part in the dance of a relationship is one of the most empowering choices I have made over the years.

There is power in taking ownership of my life. As I take radical responsibility for my actions, emotions, and thoughts, I'm able to create the life I want to experience. I no longer blame others for my bad attitude or a bad day. I practice noticing what is going on for me and focus on what I can control. I notice increased creativity and vitality, no longer wasting energy on something I can't change.

My self-trust grows more and more as I recognize the beautiful way life is leading me. It hasn't happened all at once—there have been times when I've slipped back into the old, familiar patterns of deferring to others without first checking in with myself. I would feel guilty for saying what I wanted or force myself to do something even when I knew I was exhausted and needed a break.

As I continue to trust myself and follow my inner compass, the choices I make in life are made with ease and joy. I've learned to be discerning about others' advice along this path. Some advice is worthy of attention; some is best ignored. As I make my own choices based on my inner wisdom, I demonstrate that I am responsible for my own actions rather than blaming others for what happens to me. I take ownership of my energy and time and refrain from blaming others when my schedule gets too full. I take a pause and breathe before I respond to someone's request. My body helps with this. As I pay attention, I familiarize myself with my body's messages. Tension and a sense of weightedness are a sign of resistance. When my body feels calm and my posture is relaxed, these are clues to saying yes to the next steps.

I am here to tell you that you, too, have the wisdom within to trust yourself and move forward even in the midst of uncertainty.

UNCERTAINTY

Navigating the Trail of Uncertainty

You likely know people who love the excitement of not knowing what will happen next, who get bored with routine and thrive on unexpected change and sudden upheaval. Changing jobs or moving to a new city fills them with anticipation and an eagerness to see what's next. They adjust to new situations and are able to keep healthy and vibrant in spite of the changes they are going through. It's almost as if they *like* living in the unknown.

I'm not one of those people. The trail of uncertainty is not my favourite path. I like to make plans, schedule my day, and anticipate my future. I make plans to meet a friend for coffee and look forward to our time together with excitement and joy. Then my friend cancels. Now what? Even though she has a valid reason, I get anxious. When can we book another date? What will the rest of my day look like now?

This may seem like a trivial example. But I've learned over the years that how I do the little things in life is how I do the big things.

When I am in the midst of a transition, it can feel like a big deal. Transitions create upheaval and fear because of the uncertainty they bring with them. Transitions are times that are filled with questions about what happens next. Transitions are part of the human experience.

William Bridges has written extensively about change and transition. He differentiates between the two. He states that change is the outer event that is visible and obvious. For example, when I retired from my career in healthcare, the outer event was me leaving my job and retiring. That was the event that was visible to others. Transition was something else. It was what was going on inside of me, the personal journey that only I was aware of. My full-time job had ended. I was in the middle of not knowing what was next. The beginning of my new life had not started and this created upheaval and anxiety within me.

I had a lot of questions as I moved from having a regular job to staying home and receiving a pension. I wondered what my identity would become. Would I find interests to keep me engaged in life? In this time of transition, I hardly recognized myself. I was restless, exhausted, and irritable. I was used to being focused and organized with my schedule and projects. Leaving a regular schedule caused me anxiety. I wasn't used to the idea of going through each day with no externally imposed plan. I wanted to have some certainty in my life, and things felt anything but. I remembered a metaphor of a trapeze artist suspended in the air, letting go of one ring and reaching out to grasp the next. What an image of letting go, of uncertainty, of total surrender! That's how that time felt. I'd let go of one ring and hadn't yet caught the next.

With the passing of time and my coach's support, I adjusted. I practiced self-care and learned patience for my turbulent emotions. The time of uncertainty opened up possibilities, and I realized that transition can bring gifts into my world.

Transitions can happen at any stage of life. We experience them throughout, in graduating, getting married, getting divorced, having a baby, battling a serious health issue, or supporting aging parents. The good news is you're supported and not alone. You have company on this trail of uncertainty.

Embrace Chaos

I'd been in public health nursing for many years but felt restless and eager to find another position. The programs I loved were being phased out and the job was becoming more clinical. I applied and was turned down for a position as a supervisor. Then I failed to be chosen for a clinical nurse educator role. I searched for more job openings and kept trying. The answers kept coming back. No. Not you. Not for this job. Not at this time.

The path ahead disappeared. Where did it go? A moment ago, it was clear and well-worn—I had a job and knew it well. Now all I saw were fallen logs and undergrowth. Should I turn back?

I lost my sense of confidence and wondered if I had made a mistake. Was I supposed to stay where I was? What was wrong with me? Many nurses would be content to keep the job I had. It was considered one of the best in the field. What more did I want? I was riddled with doubt and anxiety. But I forged ahead.

The many job rejections pointed to my sense of failure. What could I do next? I had tears and a deep hurt in my heart. I felt angry that there was no sense of direction in my life. The purpose I thought I had was no longer possible. The aspects of the job that I enjoyed were being phased out. Instead of facilitating parent groups and visiting new families in their homes, we were increasing the number of weekly immunization clinics, and follow-up was being done by phone. The focus on personal interactions with clients and group teaching was no longer a priority, which was a huge loss for me. This was a dead end with no options in sight, a trail that leads to a mess of mud and brambles.

The thing is, I didn't like sitting in a place of not knowing. Uncertainty was stressful for me. I had trouble focusing on my work and lost interest in creating new projects or being excited about the programs I was involved in. It seemed pointless to put energy into something I wouldn't be around to see happen. I was distracted as I daydreamed about potential new jobs. I wasn't sleeping well, got impatient with things that usually didn't bother me, and wasn't much fun to be around.

I wanted to know what to do next and the answer wasn't evident. I came to realize that learning to wait with patience was what I was being called to do. In the midst of all this, something unexpected happened.

When I was willing to stay in this place of "not knowing," I began to imagine other possibilities. Letting go of my specific plans opened up the way to other options. The chaos encouraged me to think outside the box and turn my ideas upside down in much the same way that chaos precedes new growth in nature.

UNCERTAINTY

A couple of years ago in Alberta, a forest fire destroyed many acres of Waterton Lakes National Park. In celebration of our wedding anniversary, my husband and I wanted to hike the trails we'd enjoyed on our honeymoon. We'd heard about the fires and seen the news reports, but the reality of the widespread devastation shocked us. The trails we'd been hoping to hike again no longer existed. Disappointed, we had to find other areas that were open to exploring.

The few trails we were able to walk along showed life after the fire. Trees with blackened bark were still standing. Wildflowers sprouted new life along the path. The following spring, new species of flowers were reportedly discovered in the park, having taken root and bloomed as a result of the environmental changes. This wouldn't have happened without the chaos of the fires.

I experienced this in my search for a new job. I kept my ears open for new opportunities. I took some courses in workshop facilitation and leadership development. I enrolled in a program about self-care and communication. I started practicing self-compassion and being gentle with myself. Instead of isolating myself from others, I reached out to close colleagues and told them about my struggles as I applied for new positions and kept getting rejected and saw myself as inadequate. My colleagues listened with empathy and encouraged me to be patient. They reminded me of the good work I was doing while I went through this tough time and accepted me even when I showed up subdued and reflective rather than my usual smiling self.

I knew I was not alone in this time of upheaval. Throughout my life, I've been open to working with a therapist or coach during times of transition, and this time was no different. She asked me questions that guided me to get clear on what I desired. She helped me to see my strengths in the midst of the chaos I was experiencing. She saw me as being able to move through uncertainty with trust that all would be well. Because of her coaching, I gained a new perspective on my situation.

She celebrated with me when I told her about the support I was getting from the nurses in my workplace. She reminded me I could see this as an opportunity to trust in the future, even when the trail seemed to be going nowhere. I was filled with hope and, because of her wise help, I started working on a new project. If I was going to be in this job, I wanted to make the best of it. I kept going along this trail that seemed to be a dead-end.

Then, another trail opened up for me unexpectedly.

I received a call from a former colleague who was leading a team in the area of leadership development. Several months earlier she and I had talked over lunch about the possibility of my working on her team. At that time, there were no openings.

She asked if I was still interested in a position. A team member had resigned and there was a spot open. I had a deep knowing that this was the next step for me. All the past disappointments lost their sting. In that moment, I trusted that everything I had been through was for a reason and I was being prepared for what was to come. I was able to step back and see the benefit of the lessons that the rough times of the past had for me. I was excited and thankful for this new opportunity.

There were unexpected challenges as I began my new job. There were steep climbs and hidden switchbacks. I wondered if I would have the ability to fulfill the expectations of this new position. At the same time, I noticed the exciting vistas ahead. I became a student again as I enrolled in courses to prepare me for the work I would be doing. I

UNCERTAINTY

felt energetic and enthusiastic as I studied and then taught what I had learned. I saw how my years of nursing experience had prepared me for this and how I had the skills I needed for the job.

When I am hiking and the trail disappears, I often find it helpful to stop and rest. I take stock of what my options are. I think about what step is next. Should I turn around and try another path? What about asking others if they've gone this way before? Checking in with other hikers is a way of researching and making an informed decision about whether to continue. Stopping to reflect on upcoming steps isn't wasting time.

Life is sure to be filled with times of uncertainty and messiness. When I choose to trust that chaos gives life to creativity and I move forward on the unseen path, I often find an unexpected gift awaits me.

Await Unexpected Gifts

We were ready to head home after a family vacation in Banff. It was early in the morning, and our three children were in their car seats with their stuffed animals and toys to keep them occupied on the road trip.

We packed everything up and put it in the trunk. But the trunk wouldn't close; the latch was broken. We would have to change our plans. My husband dropped me and the children off at a local restaurant while he found a repair shop.

The children and I sat at a big table. We coloured on the paper placemats as we waited for the food—pancakes with maple syrup and strawberries. It was a noisy, messy time once the food arrived. I juggled glasses of juice and cut up pancakes for the children. Syrup landed on laps and everyone wanted my help at once. I did what needed to be done, knowing it was up to me to meet their needs.

My husband and I didn't typically take the kids to a restaurant on our own, but this was an exceptional occasion. I sipped my coffee, now cold, and watched my children dig into their special breakfast. I hoped the car would be fixed soon but was happy we were in a restaurant rather than sitting at the side of the highway.

I wiped off sticky fingers and faces and took some toys out of our travel bag. As I was finishing up, I heard a voice behind me. "What a wonderful mother you are!" I turned around and saw a friendly, gray-haired woman smiling as she stood by our table. "I'm amazed at your patience and kindness with your three little children. You're doing a great job as a mom."

This loving comment caught me off guard. I didn't know anyone had been watching me! Hearing a compliment like this, out of the blue, I hardly knew what to say. I smiled and said, "Thank you," and off she went. I sat there, realizing I had tears in my eyes.

What just happened?

I had been the recipient of an unexpected gift when I chose to say yes to an unanticipated adventure and to look for the fun in the challenge of breakfast on my own with three young children. In that moment, I accepted the woman's gift fully and received her comments as truth. She witnessed me in that moment and was a mirror for and reflection of who I am.

She was an angel to me that day, encouraging me along in one of the most challenging jobs in the world. I felt validated and observed myself as a mother. Plenty of times, I didn't like how I showed up as a mother. I'd go to bed at night thinking of how I'd been tired, impatient, or short-tempered with my lively, rambunctious, energetic children. It's all too easy to focus on how I was "not enough" in this role. Was it possible that I was a patient, loving, fun mom? Maybe I was doing a good job. And what a surprise to be reminded of this in the middle of an unexpected detour.

This woman helped me see myself more fully: a mother capable of caring for her children on her own when necessary and having a playful, loving time doing so. Her comment has stayed with me for over thirty-five years. Discouraging moments still happen, but I've never forgotten what she told me, and I am inspired and moved by this memory every time I think of it.

I doubt this woman remembers this event. I sometimes wish I could meet her again and tell her what our interaction meant to me. I don't even know her name. What I do know is I want to be that kind of woman. I want to notice what's going on and encourage others by telling them what I see. I want to be part of life's gift exchange. What do I mean by "gift exchange"?

In life, I sometimes give and sometimes receive. As I receive, I show respect to the person offering a gift. A gift is not a gift unless it is received. I hold the gift in high esteem when I accept it graciously.

I know when I received that woman's gift so many years ago, she was also given one. I'm sure our brief encounter left her feeling happy too.

I think about all the people whose lives I've touched. What do they remember about me? Have I given them encouragement? Do they feel stronger and happier after seeing me? I may never know. I want to trust that my presence lifts their spirits and supports them in living more fully.

When my husband joined us at the restaurant, he too became part of the gift exchange. I told him what had happened as he ate his pancakes. He was so happy for me, and we celebrated the beautiful moment together as well as the news that the trunk lock was fixed. Soon we were on our way with light hearts, grateful for the surprising gifts life brings in the midst of the unforeseen adventures we go through.

Be Present

It had been a while since I'd taken a day to focus on writing my book. I'd been looking forward to a day to myself without coffee meetings, grandchildren to take care of, phone calls, or errands.

UNCERTAINTY

My day started with a quiet meditative ritual, writing in my journal, and setting an intention for the day. I headed out for a walk on the nearby trails, listened to the birds, and took in the fresh morning spring air.

After my shower, I felt it was time to get started, so I sat at my laptop eager for creative ideas to find me. Yet nothing came. So I waited. And waited.

What was happening?

I had a book to write. I began to feel restless and anxious. What if I didn't get any writing done today? Or tomorrow? My mind started spinning into the future. I imagined I'd never get a book written if I continued to have nonproductive days like this one. I may as well give up on this goal of mine.

Who did I think I was writing about uncertainty and guiding my readers on this trail? I couldn't even deal with the uncertainty of what might happen if I didn't write today.

Frustrated, I thought, well, if I'm not writing, I may as well do something useful. So I started cleaning. I scrubbed the bathroom, then dusted the bedroom. I noticed how exhausted I felt, physically and emotionally. I was dragging myself from one task to the next. What was going on? Why was I so tired?

Scouring the kitchen sink, I kept thinking, I should be writing. I shouldn't be wasting time cleaning. This day was supposed to be a writing day. Grumpy and irritable, I felt resentful that I "had" to clean. Why was housework my job?

Reluctantly, I reminded myself that when I fully focus on an activity, I enjoy it more. Making a pot of homemade soup becomes a meditative experience when it's what I put all my focus into. I smell the onions and garlic and rhythmically chop carrots and potatoes. I inhale the aromas and breathe in the pleasure of creating a healthy meal.

Could I do this with housework? What if I were to accept the reality that, for now, my focus was fully on cleaning? What might happen if I let go of the pressure to write at this moment?

I opened the windows and doors and cranked up some blues, my favourite music for cleaning. I breathed deeply and chose to be fully present. I took my time and noticed the pieces I was dusting, admiring the sheen of our antique dresser's dark wood. I rearranged our grandchildren's photos on the window sill, smiling as I looked at each precious face.

I felt renewed energy, my shoulders no longer tense and my body feeling light as I danced to the music. I was surprised at what a difference my attitude shift could have on not only my emotional but also my physical state. I cleaned with ease, treated myself to a leisurely lunch, and took a nap.

When I woke up, I was eager to write and feeling focused. I made a fresh pot of coffee and allowed the words to flow as I sat at my computer. I was encouraged to notice that taking a break from writing hadn't dried up my creativity. In fact, just the opposite had happened.

Following the rhythms of my energy hasn't always been easy. I've often felt uncertain I can take breaks, wondering if I'd ever resume something once I'd stopped. So I'd push myself to get things done, ignoring what my body and emotions were telling me. Not only would I miss the satisfaction of activities, but I'd be exhausted upon completion. I'd hardly notice what I was doing, just wanting to get it done as soon as possible.

I used to pride myself on how many tasks I could manage at once. Multitasking was my superpower. I couldn't imagine slowing down to focus on one task at a time. I have since learned that I actually get more tired when I do too many things at once, and I don't enjoy any of them. I rush to get them done and don't pay attention to what I'm doing. Now I do things more intentionally, slowly, and methodically, one task at a time. At first, I was uncertain I was doing enough or if it would all get done. I've learned the opposite is true. When I am present, I have more energy to get through my tasks with ease and joy. I also realize, for as much as I love to-do lists, not all tasks must be done today, and I can trust the choices I make in the moment.

Being focused on one thing at a time allows me to experience life's tasks with greater ease, whether housework, writing, work, or childcare. When I breathe deeply, focus, and accept that I'm doing exactly what's right for me in the moment, things shift in a positive direction.

Accept What Is

"It's not fair!"

"It's my turn!"

"Why can't I stay up late too?"

These were common refrains as my husband and I cared for our three grandchildren for six days. The idea that "life isn't always fair" wasn't an easy concept for them to accept.

It's not only my grandchildren who struggle with this—I do too!

While taking care of them, we discovered a water leak behind our washing machine. Our home was in upheaval. Everything seemed to be falling apart. The walls were filled with water; the hardwood floor was ruined. Areas of the house had to be sealed off against mold. Every room was outfitted with huge fans that reproduced airport ambience with their jet engine noise. My home was no longer a place of peaceful retreat.

Life was overflowing with uncertainty. I worried about all the work ahead and the many unanswered questions. When would the restoration work be done? Would insurance cover the costs? How could we celebrate Christmas in this mess? Where would we live during the cleanup and repairs? Life isn't fair! Why was this happening to me? Why now? I struggled with feelings of anger, sadness, and anxiety.

I remembered something I'd told my young granddaughter days prior when she was crying loudly, complaining about how unfair life was. She had wanted the window seat in the car and her sister got there first. She didn't want to accept her seat in the middle and wondered when she'd get her turn.

I told her, "It's okay to be sad and to cry. But there's a time to stop the tears and take some deep breaths." She was able to stop crying and settle her emotions with some slow, deep breathing. Minutes later, she was contented and happy. She was also delighted to hear that the window seat would be hers on the way home.

UNCERTAINTY

Could I apply this to myself? I'd spent several days feeling frustrated and upset. Some quotes by Pema Chodron from a favourite book of mine came to mind. She writes:

"The healing comes from letting there be room for all of this to happen: room for grief, for relief, for misery, for joy."

My resistance wouldn't change the reality of the situation. What might happen if I allowed my sadness to be present? What if I could admit the loss I felt when my home wasn't a place of peace and beauty? In the midst of not knowing what will happen next, could I trust and be with my messy emotions? What if I let go of feeling resentful and thinking the water leak was unfair?

Over time, reflecting on these ideas, I chose to accept my situation, even if I wasn't sure how it could help me find joy and contentment. Another reminder from Pema Chodron's book helped me reframe what was going on. "When there's a big disappointment, we don't know if that's the end of the story. It may be just the beginning of a great adventure."

Acceptance is a word I often think of when I'm in a place of upset or wanting direction in life. It is a stance of strength. It's not a sign of weakness. Acceptance signifies choice rather than resignation and victimhood. What does it look like when I choose to practice acceptance as I navigate times of uncertainty? When I accept what happens, I focus my energy on what I have control over. I release my anxious thoughts about details that are unknown and out of my control.

Uncertainty by its very nature invites me to worry. I'm learning ways to overcome my anxiety, such as putting my focus on my attitude. I look for what I can be grateful for and remind myself to imagine the possibility of adventure ahead. I pay attention to the people around me who show me love and on whom I can rely for support. This often means stopping to breathe deeply, just as I encouraged my granddaughter to do. The intensity of my fear lessens, and I'm more calm and hopeful.

How might this be relevant to my flooded home?

I think about my attitude and choose to focus on gratitude rather than grumbling and complaining. I'm thankful for our house insurance that covers the renovation and temporary accommodation costs. I'm thankful no furniture or belongings were ruined. I appreciate my husband's leadership in communicating with the tradespeople and insurance adjustor. A skilled woodworker, he knows the right questions to ask. As I shift my attitude, I feel lighter and see myself as strong and capable rather than a victim.

Meanwhile, I created a space of beauty in an area that was unaffected by the leak. A Christmas tree aglow with lights and decorations, candles lit, and music filled the room. I planned a gathering of friends at our home, even in the midst of the chaos. Instead of unfinished walls and piled-up boxes, home would mean good food, conversation, and love.

Acceptance is a mindset I can choose to embody no matter what happens in life. Uncertainty necessarily shows up one way or another. I want to remember the power of accepting what's happening and focusing on what I have control over when I'm faced with upheaval and messy times. When I embody acceptance, I am able to shift from anger and resentment to surrender and trust.

UNCERTAINTY

Surrender and Let Go

One day, after weeks of rain, the sun was shining. I was excited to walk in the woods on a clear, crisp spring morning. I laced up my shoes and headed out.

But then I noticed it. A flat tire. This wasn't how I'd imagined my day. I was going to meet a friend for lunch after my walk and would need my car. I wanted to get it fixed as soon as possible.

So instead of enjoying my date with Mother Nature, I phoned the automobile association for help. I caught myself muttering about how there was nothing for me to do but wait. I was sure it would be hours before they arrived. I could feel my impatience as I rubbed my tight shoulder muscles and noticed my clenched jaw. I was not in the mood to let go of my schedule for the day. It didn't matter that I coached others about surrendering to events out of our control. I was upset.

That's when I got another surprise. This one brought a smile to my face.

The tow truck arrived in under twenty minutes. I breathed a sigh of relief and welcomed the driver, thanking him for arriving so quickly and chatting about his work. I realized his job was often dangerous and thankless. He quickly and cheerfully put on a spare tire. I was inspired by his expertise and the pleasure he showed in helping, filled with gratitude for people like him who do so much to keep others safe.

I drove to the tire shop where my flat tire was quickly repaired and was all set to go. I shared the story with my friend over lunch and was struck by the ease and flow surrounding me as I dealt with what could have been a major upset. She wondered what caused my shift from impatience to acceptance. I had to stop and think about that and became aware of how my attitude changed when I expressed gratitude to the tow truck driver. Being in the energy of appreciation made it impossible for me to feel angry and upset. I started noticing what else was going well for me in the midst of this unexpected event, including the efficient, friendly service at the tire shop. And, now I was enjoying the connection with a dear friend over lunch. My day had not turned out as planned, and as I let go of my expectations, I was filled with appreciation and joy. All was well.

After my lunch date, my mind was drawn to something that had been weighing on my heart. Little did I know that I was about to experience another opportunity to receive the gifts that follow when I let go and surrender to the unknown.

I'd been thinking about visiting my parents in Winnipeg for some weeks. I liked to visit them regularly, but several months had passed since my last visit, and I knew I didn't want to wait much longer.

At ninety-four, my mother was physically and mentally frail. She didn't always recognize her children, and the dark days outnumbered the light ones. I was grieving the loss of the mother I no longer had. I felt a strong sense to book a flight for some time in the next few weeks. The precariousness of her health created an urgency in me to visit soon.

But the unpredictability of the future also caused me hesitation. So many unknowns lay ahead. Leaving on this trip didn't fit with the plans I had.

UNCERTAINTY

I was afraid of leaving my coaching business and losing momentum if I went away for a week. I didn't know if I could reschedule client sessions or the women's circles I led. Would I have enough time to prepare for the retreat I was hosting in less than a month? How could I leave with all of this uncertainty in my life? Could I let go of the pressure to be constantly working on my business? Surrendering the high standard I had for myself meant giving myself permission to take a break from my work schedule. It also meant letting go of what others might think of me if I rescheduled appointments.

I listened to my inner wisdom and heard my heart say, "Go."

I took the leap and decided to fly to Winnipeg. I let go of my worries and surrendered to the voice in my heart.

Then magic happened yet again. I called my travel agent and dear friend. She effortlessly booked my flights. Completing the transaction, she noted, "Oh, you got the last seat." What a heartwarming "coincidence." As I surrendered to whatever would happen instead of worrying about the timing of my trip or if it was too expensive, I discovered the gift of lightness and ease in what could have been an otherwise stressful process.

There are times when I don't even know what I want to have happen next. All I know is that I don't like how things are in that moment. When that happens, I remind myself to let go of my need for certainty. I sit with the discomfort of not knowing. I find this challenging, but certain actions, such as deep breathing or walking in nature, help support me when the trail ahead winds through the swamp of uncertainty and everything seems dark and hopeless. I trust the journey will continue even in the messiness of an unmarked trail and unfamiliar surroundings.

That's what surrender looks like for me—letting go of what I think should be and embracing what is. I believe I'm exactly where I'm meant to be at this moment. All will be well even if I can't see the way clearly. My job is to keep hiking, to surrender and let go of my insistence on a certain destination or type of terrain. It's up to me to be with what is rather than thinking things should be different.

Only when I accept the reality of an uncharted future can I surrender to the unknown. The path ahead may be overgrown with underbrush, obscuring what lies around a curve in the trail, but I must let go of needing to see the whole picture and courageously take one step at a time. As I accept the discomfort of not knowing or the disappointment of what is, I develop a sense of trust. Because of my past experiences and taking time to reflect that everything worked out for the best, I can surrender more and more to what will be.

When I approach my day with curiosity and openness to what may happen rather than grasping and clinging to a rigid list of events, I'm more relaxed. I plan my day knowing there may be unexpected things in store. It could be a flat tire, a traffic jam, or a slow line at the grocery store. Instead of fuming and telling myself something shouldn't happen to me, I breathe deeply and let go of my expectations, surrendering to what is. Living with uncertainty can become an adventure when I choose love and gratitude for what shows up along the trail.

The little things in life add up to the major daily shifts in attitude and approach. It's an epiphany to celebrate, one step at a time. One action each moment. Being aware of the choice of how to experience an event. Looking for clues to encourage me on my path to joy, love, and living authentically.

UNCERTAINTY

I am no longer the Marjorie who manages at all costs, feeling I need to control each and every outcome. I am the Marjorie who trusts herself to embrace the uncertainty of life deeply and authentically. I am not a victim of my circumstances. From this place of love and self-compassion, I see myself in a favourable light attracting all kinds of abundance and relationships to support me along this magical and, at times, messy trail called life.

Living authentically requires me to be at peace with what life brings me.

AUTHENTICITY

Exploring the Trail of Living Authentically

―――▶

Leading workshops, I'd hear participants say, "I'm not an emotional person. I don't do feelings. I'm a thinker; feelings aren't part of my personality."

Everyone has feelings whether they know it or not. In fact, research shows that many decisions are made based on feelings rather than logic or facts. Brain scans show that decision-making begins in the emotional part of the brain, which lights up before the thinking part does. This is often unconscious and is a fascinating insight into emotions and how human beings make choices.

Many of us have a limited vocabulary when it comes to naming emotions. Once we recognize and name our feelings, we have the knowledge to choose how to be with them. When we act upon our feelings from a place of knowledge, we have the power to create the life we want.

The ability to be real with my emotions is the gateway to living authentically. The first step is for me to be aware of what I am feeling so that I can process it. I felt sad and weepy on the one-year anniversary of my mother's death and allowed myself to grieve. I took the day to myself, walking in the woods and sitting by the river to reflect on my mother's love. I have learned to describe what I am feeling so that others know what is going on for me and then allow it to flow through me. Not only does this lead to improved health and peace in my body and mind, but it also allows me to be authentic in my relationships.

Learning to release shame is another key component of living authentically, and my ability to talk about my shame to someone I trust is a key part of that process. In order to have the courage to face my shame and share it, I must see myself as worthy of doing so. This is where self-compassion becomes important.

Self-compassion means that I am kind to myself in the midst of unsettling emotions. I am actually suffering when I feel grief, anger, or shame. It's important neither to diminish nor over-emphasize the impact of my suffering. I can't comfort myself if I ignore my pain.

When I actively comfort myself, I practice self-care and experience more pleasure. Caring for myself is foundational to living authentically. I have nothing to give to others unless I am replenished and overflowing with love and joy, and this happens when I pay attention to my needs. I am not being selfish when I put myself first. I have learned that play and pleasure enrich not only my life but the lives of those around me. It could be as simple as taking a break at my favourite coffee shop and reading a novel or building a Lego project with my grandson. Play is not a waste of time, and, in fact, research shows that play clears the mind, increases productivity, and leads to enjoyment of life.

AUTHENTICITY

Living authentically requires me to be at peace with what life brings me. When upsets happen along the path, I have more emotional resilience and patience with unexpected falls or detours. I have learned practices to manage those moments in the dark of night when I suffer from once-overwhelming fears. I speak kindly to myself and remind myself that I'm not alone in this shared human experience.

Feel My Feelings

I got up on the wrong side of the bed one day. Grumpy, tired, and out of sorts, I felt nothing was going right. I was overwhelmed with my writing projects and saw myself as useless and a failure.

I was tempted to skip my regular morning walk in the woods, but I went out reluctantly and started walking. Fast. I muttered as I walked, pushing myself to pound the trails at top speed. Why couldn't I cheer up? Why didn't I sleep better? What was wrong with me? The sun was shining, the birds were singing, and I was still upset. How ungrateful could I be? What if my mood prevented me from getting anything done that day? How could I even hope to write a page, let alone a whole book?

I felt tears on my face. My heart was in turmoil. I stopped and allowed the tears to fall. I found a tree near the trail and wrapped my arms around its rough bark. I laid my cheek against the trunk and more tears flowed. I listened to the tree, allowing my breath to slow and deepen.

I kept walking and made a choice. I would feel all the messy emotions for a bit longer. Then, when I got to a crosswalk, I would view it as a portal to a new experience. I would be on the lookout for love and beauty along my walk.

I crossed the road.

The greens were brighter. The birds sang louder and more sweetly. I slowed my pace and breathed in the scent of wild roses. Newborn ducklings paddled awkwardly in the pond as their mothers hovered close by.

Even the people walking by me seemed friendlier. There was an older gentleman with a little dog, and I stopped to say hello. The dog's name was TJ, his owner smilingly told me. "Tiny Joy," he explained, "has been my companion since my wife died last year." I patted the dog and said with a soft heart, "How wonderful that you have each other."

As I walked on, I felt such joy and gratitude for my life. Here was a glowing example of someone who saw the best in life and shared his joy freely.

Allowing the grief and upsetting emotions to flow through me and be released offered me the gift of this man's presence. In the past, I worried that doing so might cause negative emotions to worsen, always doing my utmost to ignore, numb, or push away my sadness or anger. I was afraid that the intensity of my anger would get so strong that I'd lose control and maybe even hurt someone physically or emotionally. If I let myself cry, could I ever stop? I might become a neurotic, unbalanced woman with no self-control. I worried my emotions would take over and consume me. What if I became depressed or volatile? It was safer for me to hide my strong feelings and pretend they weren't there.

AUTHENTICITY

As a young girl, I was taught to keep calm and control my feelings. Crying and throwing temper tantrums were what my little brothers and sisters could get away with. I was the oldest; I knew better than to act out. In my desire to please my parents, I took pride in being calm, cool, and collected—demonstrating my ability to maintain peace, unlike my younger siblings. In fact, I often took on the role of keeping them in line and scolding them if they fought or cried. I wanted to be a good girl, and that meant keeping my emotions in check as well as those of my brothers and sisters.

In later years, I admired my nursing leaders who kept their heads in an emergency and never raised their voices. This was the sign of a competent, in-charge person, someone who could be counted on to manage a crisis and prevent a potential tragedy. I applied this standard to myself even when I was away from work, managing and controlling my feelings.

As I distracted myself from my emotions over the years, I thought they would disappear. But no—they remained in my body until, eventually, I noticed signs of chronic stress. I suffered from headaches, shoulder tension, upset stomach, and low energy due to poor sleep from anxiety and worry.

Thanks to my coach, books, and retreats, I started hearing about the process of feeling my feelings and saw examples of others freely expressing all kinds of emotions. I saw the healing and lightness that resulted as they allowed whatever came up to move through them.

With practice and a lot of courage, I started expressing my emotions. I cried and let tears wash away my sadness. The concept of "having a good cry" started to make sense. I admitted when I was angry and vented to my husband or journal. I started being open about what was upsetting me instead of pretending nothing was wrong.

As I allowed emotions to flow through me, I started feeling healthier. Many studies show the correlation between illness and repressed emotions. As I learn to acknowledge and express my feelings, my body is less stressed. My back and shoulder muscles relax and my jaw unclenches. It's a practice that takes patience and continues to this day. It's a vulnerable act to admit when I'm scared or sad.

Here's the thing. If I'm afraid of feeling these feelings, I won't try anything new. My ability to move forward is related to my capacity to sit with sadness, doubt, and uncomfortable feelings. Fully acknowledging my feelings leads to greater awareness and power. As they pass through me, I'm able to emerge with a sense of possibility and purpose.

It's even harder for me to celebrate loudly and take up space when I am excited. For so long, I've felt that I'm "too much," perceiving myself as boastful and arrogant when my accomplishments are recognized. It goes back to a false idea of humility and a lack of understanding the power of owning my gifts and celebrating myself. I wonder if it's tied to my religious upbringing, which warned me about the danger of pride. Humility was the goal, which I interpreted as downplaying my abilities. This attitude is the exact opposite of authenticity.

When I live authentically, I am true to myself and give myself the freedom to say yes to all of who I am. I am learning to experience my full range of emotions. No longer stuffing down the darker feelings of sadness, anger, or anxiety or the "too much" emotions of celebration, I accept myself with love as I express all of it.

I don't want to go back to pretending nothing bothers me, acting as if I'm doing fine when I feel I'm falling apart. I love the freedom of being myself and showing up authentically. I used to keep my sadness tucked away. No more. I no longer hesitate to tell my husband that I'm mourning my mother's memory loss. I'm willing to admit my grief, which means he's able to comfort me. I can be myself around my family. If I'm physically weary or feeling overwhelmed with the grandchildren's exuberance, I tell them I need a break.

The key is to focus on what I'm feeling rather than any sense of failure. Stepping back and noticing my experience with more authenticity and less shame, I'm able to put it into perspective. Because I'm genuine with my feelings, they know what I'm going through and are more than willing to make sure I get what I need. I accept the support of those who care for me and remember I'm not alone.

Release Shame

I love a prairie thunderstorm! Dark clouds rolling in across the big sky announce the dramatic display that's on its way. Flashes of lightning are followed by the crashing of thunder reverberating over the fields. Then the rain starts pelting down, the huge drops hitting the ground in a symphony of sound.

On a road trip to Winnipeg, my husband and I encountered a storm. Except it wasn't a thunderstorm. There wasn't a cloud in the sky on this hot summer day in the prairies.

The heat waves shimmered on the highway, and we were ready to cool off when a Dairy Queen came into view. What a treat a soft vanilla cone and hot fudge sundae would be. A perfect rest stop.

We finished our ice cream, and I offered to take a turn at the wheel. I got into the driver's seat and started the car. Turning to Al, I asked, "Which way do I go?" He looked at me in disbelief. "How can you ask that? There aren't many roads going to Winnipeg."

The storm was rolling in. I call this one a shame storm.

It was instantly obvious that I was a failure. Useless. A complete idiot. How could I be so stupid?

My throat grew dry and my cheeks flushed. This time not because of the hot weather. My heart was racing, my stomach was in knots, and my hands were clenched around the steering wheel.

I huffed my way out of the car declaring, "Okay, you drive." I stomped over to the passenger seat and glared at Al as he got out of the car. I got in, slammed the door shut, and sat there steaming. I dreaded another two days of driving together. Wanting to disappear, I shut down emotionally.

I felt angry at Al, but not as mad as I was at myself. I withdrew and felt critical. What was wrong with me? Why couldn't I be more kind? I started thinking there isn't any hope for me to be a loving person. I imagined other people didn't struggle with directions like I do. Something within me must be faulty and unworthy. I forgot my authentic nature.

This was several years ago before I had learned about shame and its impact on me. I came to learn that when my shame is triggered as it was that day, my relationship with myself and others suffers a breakdown. Wallowing in the swamp of shame, I wasn't living authentically. I would pretend all is okay, and the pretending would take its toll. The stress would then lead to illness and unhappiness in my relationships until I admitted what was actually happening.

AUTHENTICITY

Shame is the view of myself as unworthy of love, intrinsically bad, and useless. It isn't based on anything I've done that I should be sorry for. Guilt, on the other hand, can be a useful emotion, as it reminds me of when I've done something harmful or inconsiderate. I can then apologize or fix whatever mistakes I made.

I now understand there's nothing wrong about not knowing which direction to go. Many people depend on others for directions without shame. They are willing to admit they need help and continue along.

That's the thing about shame—it's a unique and individual experience.

In preparation for workshops I've taught on this topic and moving through these times personally, I have found resources that offer practical ways to release the shame that shows up in life. *Clear Leadership* by Gervase Bushe and *The Gifts of Imperfection* by Brené Brown are invaluable resources that come to mind.

The first step toward releasing shame is to notice and admit when it's present. Physical symptoms are a clue. My throat grows dry and my cheeks flush. My heart races, my stomach ties up in knots, and my hands clench. Whatever it is you notice from your body, pay attention. This will help take you to the next step.

These times of difficulty are also an opportunity for acceptance and compassion. Reaching out for help is crucial, and it's one of the hardest things for me to do when my shame causes such self-hatred. Help seems like an unrealistic expectation. Who would want to be with me when I'm *such* a loser?

Sharing is a vulnerable act that takes courage. I am inspired by Brené Brown's words, "Shame can't live in the light of vulnerability." It shrivels up like a sand crab scurrying out of the sun when I lift the rock above it.

If I want to release my shame and be authentic, I must find someone I trust and tell them my story. Not just anyone. I have a select few people in my life whom I trust to hear me out when I'm in a shame storm. They accept me in all my messiness and listen with empathy and compassion. They don't give advice or try to match my story with their own. As they show acceptance of who I am by being in my darkness with me, I can release the shameful image of myself and show up as me.

As I tell my story, my trusted friend reminds me to let my emotions out. I let the tears flow and give myself permission to be upset. I remind myself that I'm worthy of love, that I'm not that horrible person I envisioned during my shame, and I raise my arms high and laugh out loud. I am loved. I am enough as I am. I can be my authentic self, and I will travel this path with lightness and courage.

Shame can happen unexpectedly. The practice of self-compassion is essential along the challenging, yet rewarding trail of facing and moving past shame. As I release shame, I show myself love and grace as I would a close friend, saying, "You are worthy of love and belonging."

Practice Self-Compassion

Over lunch at my favourite garden cafe, a dear friend asked, "Do you ever feel like a hamster on a wheel going nowhere quickly? Where your mind is spinning and it seems impossible to stop the thoughts whirling around in your head?"

AUTHENTICITY

I took another bite and gave myself a moment.

"Yes," I admitted, "I have had times like that. Usually in the dark of the night—you know, just before dawn, three or four o'clock in the morning. When everyone else is sleeping and I'm consumed by my to-do list and worries and feelings of inadequacy."

We compared notes, sharing our experiences and similar challenges. I thought about this pattern in my life and realized that it had become less frequent over time.

What had made the difference?

In the past, whenever I felt worried and anxious, I'd grow impatient with myself, telling myself to snap out of it, scolding myself for being so weak. Why couldn't I push myself to be relaxed and happy? Look at everyone else; they seem to be managing well. What's wrong with me?

This strategy rarely worked for me, and things often, in fact, got worse as I shamed myself and amplified the negative energy already within me.

Then I was introduced to the concept of self-compassion. When I attended the first Emerging Women Conference several years ago, Kristin Neff was one of the speakers. She's a researcher who's been studying self-compassion for over ten years and authored the book *Self-Compassion*. Her website is filled with practice and theory grounded in this concept.

Self-compassion is treating myself with kindness instead of hurling judgment at myself. It includes self-comfort, which seemed awkward at first. Though I was good at encouraging and supporting others, extending warmth and understanding to myself was new to me. I practiced the art of speaking to myself as I would to a friend in need of comfort. I even hugged myself and whispered soothing endearments. I acknowledged my suffering and changed my self-talk from contempt to kindness when I felt pain or disappointment.

I was intrigued by the research showing how this practice releases oxytocin, the feel-good hormone. I saw proof when I acted kindly and warmly to myself. I felt calm and secure, my thoughts no longer spinning on the hamster wheel of worry.

When I'm feeling discouraged or inadequate, it's easy for me to imagine I'm the only one in the world who's suffering. However, as Kristin Neff says, "The emotion of compassion springs from the recognition that the human experience is imperfect." Suffering is part of the shared human experience and self-compassion recognizes that. When I feel connected to others in my experience of pain, knowing I am not alone, I can live more authentically as I receive their compassion and, most importantly, offer my own.

What I've come to realize is that my sadness and shame are true suffering and must be acknowledged. I accept my reality, and I'm able to feel pain without ignoring or exaggerating it. Only then can I practice extending love to myself and accept the invitation Kristin Neff offers in her book. This quote paints a picture for me of what is possible when practicing the art and science of self-compassion.

Relax.

Allow life to be as it is.

Open your heart to yourself.

AUTHENTICITY

Care for Myself

What comes to mind when you think about self-care?

Spending a day at a luxurious spa, shopping for that perfect pair of boots, or taking a romantic vacation on a tropical island are all wonderful ways of practicing self-care. The problem is how often can you experience this type of activity?

What does taking care of yourself look like on a rainy November day when the laundry is piling up, the bills need to be paid, and the babysitter cancels last minute? Tending to yourself can easily fall to the bottom of your list of priorities at times like this. It can seem frivolous, even selfish.

In the past, when I so diligently followed the advice of the experts in my life, I felt disillusioned by the entire concept of self-care. I knew it was important but wondered if it would become yet another "should" in my already full life.

Then I met my Wise Woman and learned to trust myself and listen to what she had to say. Unless I figure out how to care for myself, I'm not truly living authentically.

I realized that I had all the wisdom I needed to start doing this. I intuitively knew that taking care of myself starts with self-awareness. I began by paying attention to how my body felt and learning which body signals meant anxiety, upset, fear, anger. The physical symptoms are clues to corresponding emotions. I named my emotions and considered what to do next. I was getting in touch with what I wanted and needed.

Recognizing desires is another important step in what's sometimes described as the "sacred act of self-care." In my coaching business, I often ask women what they want and am told, "I want my children to be safe" or "I want my partner to be happy." They aren't aware that these responses don't get at the heart of what they want for themselves. Many women struggle to put their true desires into words. Declaring what I want for myself is an act of radical courage.

As I began trusting myself, I discovered that my desires are valid and I'm worthy of aspiring for what I want. I no longer waited for circumstances to happen. I said yes to following my dreams and what I envisioned for myself. I would take action and see what happened rather than be a bystander of my life. I became willing to experiment and try new things in life. If things didn't work, I could learn from the experience and try something else. I was living authentically as I took charge of my journey to put myself first.

Just as there are seasons in nature, I experience a range of cycles emotionally. This means giving myself time to move through disappointment, grief, and loss. When my mother died, I had no interest in writing or leading women's circles. I had already been dreaming of writing a book and felt impatient with myself, thinking I should move on more quickly. Instead, I listened to my body and inner wisdom and received wise advice from my coach and dear friends. It became clear that time was what I needed. I took a year off from "doing" and paid attention to my sorrow. I didn't know how long it would take. I nurtured myself by not rushing this process, slowing down and trusting I'd know when I was ready to return to my book and coaching business.

AUTHENTICITY

I've found that sharing my sadness and frustration vulnerably is a doorway to deeper connection and the love I long for. I know that I thrive when I connect with someone who will listen without judgment. Calling a trusted friend to share with is another way of being kind to myself.

In contrast to shame, which sucks life out, self-care is sensual, creative, and life-giving. Sensuality is when I fully embrace and appreciate the experiences life offers, like the joy of time spent in nature or with friends with whom my spirit is nourished and I feel encouraged to face life's challenges.

Food is also a doorway to the sensual self. Making a big pot of soup, with the aromas filling the kitchen and the jewel-toned hues of ingredients, brings me joy. I love the juice running down my chin as I bite into a Spartan apple. Nothing beats the scent of freshly-baked chocolate chip cookies—unless maybe their intoxicating sweetness as I sneak one, still warm, from the pan, savouring each morsel. Feeding my body food that also feeds my senses is a nourishing act that I especially enjoy.

The softness of the rain on my face and the sound of crisp autumn leaves under my feet are gifts I receive from nature. Slowly easing into a warm bubble bath and floating in a space of restfulness soothes my body and soul. The sweet, sticky kisses of my little grandchildren connect me to my senses.

Self-care can also be about embracing laughter and light-hearted moments. I let go of always looking good or getting it right. Now I enjoy trying new things and exploring fun activities. Zumba classes, hiking, and swimming with my grandchildren are some of the ways I practice lightness and play. When I give loving care to myself, I experience pleasure. I feel happy and healthy and want more of those sensations in my life.

Embrace Play and Pleasure

I rocked the crib vigorously. I was nine years old, and it was the end of a scorching summer day. My little brother kept squirming and whimpering. He just wouldn't sleep. With a big sigh, I looked out the window where my friends and siblings were laughing over a lively game of croquet and enjoying the evening coolness. Here I was, stuck in a hot upstairs bedroom trying to get my baby brother to sleep while everyone else had fun. I knew my parents were counting on me to take care of him, but I wished I could be outside with the other kids. When would I get a chance to play?

The oldest child of six, I was the designated helper. I grew up in a home with no indoor plumbing or modern conveniences. Every Monday, the kitchen became the laundry room and, when I wasn't at school, I hung out the wash and folded diapers. I often watched the little ones while my mother cooked and cleaned. Saturdays were not a day off—they were for cleaning, for baking and food preparation as we got ready for Sunday.

Summer meant weeding the garden, shelling peas, and canning beets and beans for the long winter ahead. I could hear the shouts in the field nearby as the softball game started without me. In my childhood, this is what I saw and learned: Play only happens after all the work is done.

Fast forward to my adult years. Play was seldom a priority for me, especially working full time as a nurse and raising three children. There always seemed to be something that needed doing. Play seemed like a

AUTHENTICITY

frivolous waste of time. Life was serious, after all. I was a responsible adult. I needed to take care of my family and household.

I was exhausted and felt resentful on my days off. My husband was home with our children, and he took the lead on household duties. In spite of this, I pushed myself to do chores and catch up on domestic activities when I was at home.

I noticed my husband's ability to play and have fun. He would take the children swimming or to the park even if there were dirty dishes in the sink. What was he thinking? Didn't he see that there was more work to do? Didn't he realize how much needed to get done? How could he give himself permission to relax?

There were certainly times when I was critical of his choices, but I was intrigued by his ability to have fun. I saw that the chores got done eventually, and he was enjoying life along the way. Our children thrived on the sense of adventure and fun that he brought to our family, and I wanted to be included in that. I liked the idea of more lightness and play in my life. I talked with my husband about things we might do on my days off. We planned hikes and outings with our children and family friends. We booked a babysitter for date nights on a regular basis. I learned to relax about the pace at which he completed housework. If I truly trusted him to do his job as a house-husband, I could leave the dishes in the sink and get outside for a bike ride. It wasn't my responsibility to take care of all those details.

The shift didn't happen quickly. Old habits are hard to change, and this was no exception. But then I started noticing the positive results of taking time to play with my family.

I started feeling renewed and rested after a day off. I had more patience with my children and colleagues. I began planning pleasurable activities for myself, even on workdays. I would read a book on my lunch break or get outside for a short walk. I would imagine fun times for the coming evenings—a TV special or movie I'd been wanting to see, perhaps a bubble bath.

While I was getting more comfortable with play, it sometimes upset my inner critic. I could hear her telling me how lazy I was getting and that I should get more housework done. In these moments, I knew it was time for me to tell her everything was under control. She needn't worry about me. I acknowledged her care for me, and then I went out for a hike. I knew it was important to let go of my guilt even if the laundry was piled up or the sink was full of dirty dishes. I had already experienced how much better I felt when I set aside time to enjoy myself, and I intended to experience more of this in my life.

A few years ago, my husband and I treated our family to a vacation at Disneyland. While we were on this holiday, I became aware of what I call the "shadow side" of play in my life.

The rest of the family left two days before my husband and I flew home. What would the two of us do on our own? Al got all excited talking about the rides he loves and the park attractions we'd visit together—places our grandchildren hadn't been interested in that we could take our time enjoying together.

I wasn't quite as enthusiastic. I immediately thought of reasons why it wouldn't work. It would cost too much. It would be crowded and noisy. We had already had three days there; why go again? Even as I listed my reasons, I was surprised at my resistance to the idea. I was curious as to why I would hesitate to spend another day playing, especially since

AUTHENTICITY

it would be a day for just us. We were already staying the extra nights at the hotel. What would keep me from jumping at this opportunity?

I got in touch with my thoughts and feelings and discovered something about my beliefs that was new to me. I had a story that I had reached my upper limit in terms of how much play I could participate in. I thought I had had enough fun for one week. It was an unconscious belief: three days of play is all I deserve. Surely it was time to get back to work by now.

As I became aware of this, I thought about how I would have reacted to this in the past. I would have scolded myself and been critical of my lack of willingness to play. I could hear myself: "How silly can you be, Marjorie? What a spoilsport you are." It would have been a perfect shame storm.

This time, instead of shaming myself, I practiced self-compassion. I spoke kindly to myself and reminded myself that I was still learning about the freedom to play. As a little girl, I only played after my work was done. Now, I had the opportunity to play whenever and for as long as I wanted to.

I said yes to the extra day of fun. When we got to the ticket booth, we were greeted by abundance. Because we had purchased a three-day pass for our initial time at the park, the extra day cost us a fraction of what we expected to pay. For me, this was a wink from the universe that my money worries would be taken care of as I said yes to play. I had been willing to pay the extra money regardless, and this was an added gift on this extraordinary day.

What a magical adventure we had! I browsed the shops and got a pair of blue mouse-ear-shaped crystal earrings to commemorate the holiday.

We had a leisurely lunch and went back for late evening rides and a delicious treat of appetizers and drinks. Jazz music and the warm darkness added a touch of mystery and romance as we lingered long into the night. I was able to relax into the spirit of fun and loved every minute of our time together. Disneyland is not just for kids.

Play is a powerful foundation for a life filled with freedom and joy. These days, I watch my grandchildren play and am inspired to follow their lead. They're curious and eager to try new things, not comparing themselves to each other as they are fully engaged in whatever they're doing.

I think back to when I used to tell myself, "I'll play when my work is done." Often, that time never arrived. Now, I focus on cultivating a playful approach to life, which, to me, means being open to surprises and life's unexpected events. When I practice the art of play, it means I take time to notice what's around me. I look for ways I can stop and capture a light-hearted moment. I may be driving by a playground and take time to enjoy the swings or walk on the trails. I may wear a bright outfit and my sparkly Disneyland earrings. I may invite my husband to an impromptu happy hour at a new pub in town. Daydreaming is another wonderful source of pleasure I can access when I create space for quiet time and solitude.

I'm learning I can enjoy my work and have a sense of lightness at the same time, turning up the blues music while I clean, creating an outdoor space for writing, being inspired by the hummingbird at the feeder and the scent of sweet peas, or inviting my husband to grocery shop and stop at our favourite coffee shop on the way home.

With pleasure and play, I am childlike and in the moment. I worry less and am truly myself. I smile more and feel relaxed and happy. Life is

AUTHENTICITY

full of possibilities. I see the abundance around me. I notice the smiles of others and understand that they want to be with me when I show up this way. Equally, they are inspired to play and experience more pleasure and lightness in their lives.

Incorporating this into my life on a regular basis is the path to living more authentically and a significant aspect to being a true leader.

LEADERSHIP

Enjoying the Trail of Being a True Leader

Most of my life, others have seen me as a leader—someone who takes charge and whom others follow. The eldest child in the family, always taking pleasure in pleasing and helping, I did what needed to be done. I was praised for my leadership and willingness to help, and that praise kept me going.

Now I understand, while I may have looked like a leader, following the examples of experts in my life wasn't me leading from my inner wisdom. Was I really a leader? Or a follower in disguise?

What does it look like to be a true leader?

Leading from their inner wisdom makes it possible for a true leader to have a sense of purpose and clarity about what direction they are going. They are not easily influenced by criticism or others' opinions. They are secure enough in their leadership to be willing to ask for help, and they are discerning in which help they accept. A true leader is open to partnership with those who are aligned with their vision.

They step forward with confidence even though they may not know the outcome. They are willing to accept that uncertainty is part of life and to admit when they don't know the answer to something. Because they trust themselves, they take risks and accept responsibility for their actions. True leadership means taking action based on their strong convictions and the certainty that arises from their own beliefs.

A true leader engages with others from the perspective of listening and looking for the gift in everyone. This type of leader knows that each person has something to offer, and even though the gifts may be hidden, with support and encouragement, they are discovered.

When I first started trusting myself and leading from my own wisdom, I was afraid, worried I didn't have the capacity to lead from my Wise Woman. A true leader must navigate these fear blocks along the path as they learn to move forward with courage.

Unless a leader is clear about boundaries, they aren't truly leading from their inner wisdom. Boundaries are tricky. This is especially true if a leader focuses on pleasing others at all costs. A true leader keeps their goal in mind and says no to things that might get in the way of reaching that goal. There's a breathtaking view of the freedom that comes from saying no when it's a no and then being able to give a full-bodied yes when it's a yes.

Much like you have kept going on this long and, at times, arduous journey called life, a true leader hangs in there, committed to staying on course, not giving up, taking things one step at a time.

LEADERSHIP

Find the Gift in Everyone

I met Rose when she gave birth to her firstborn, a healthy baby boy. As a public health nurse, my job was to visit her at home for support with breastfeeding and other needs. Everything seemed to be going well. Tommy was growing and smiled at me when I weighed him. It was a different story for Rose. She was weepy and would lie awake at night, unable to relax, even when Tommy was sleeping. She struggled to find the energy to cook meals and had little interest in coming out to the parent and baby group at the health unit.

A group of nurses and I were on a mission to change the way we worked with our clients. We were experimenting with a new approach to working with over-burdened families. I asked Rose if I could visit her weekly. It would be a time for us to have conversations about anything she wanted. I wouldn't label her as having a problem. In fact, I would look for the gifts in her life, and she would be my partner in this. Everyone has a gift, even those diagnosed with depression.

Over a period of months, we talked about what Rose loved to do for fun. She told me about her travels with her husband and her art projects. I heard about her family who lived across the country and how much she missed her mother. I began to see her as a gifted artist, a loving wife and daughter, and a mother who wanted desperately to be healthy for her son. With time, she began to see herself as more than a mother with depression. She started going for walks with her baby and phoned her mom when she felt lonely. She began painting again, and I was encouraged to see her spirits lift as she focused on her gifts.

I met Rose many months later. She told me, "I said yes to you because I knew you weren't coming to fix my problems. You saw me as capable and loving, even if I was depressed. I'm doing so much better now, and Tommy is healthy and happy." She thanked me.

In my interactions with this new mother, I showed up as a true leader. I was acting from the gifts of my values and beliefs. We didn't ignore her depression, but we allowed her abilities to overpower the roadblocks she faced. When gifts are named, we can find a way through, under, or over roadblocks. Gifts are resources available to help us move toward solutions.

A true leader doesn't show up as an all-knowing expert. I came alongside Rose, and we sat together with the uncertainty of her depression. As she talked about herself, I listened for what was unsaid, asking questions that led her to access her own wisdom. There was no rule book or rigid program for her to follow. I was comfortable with the messiness and uncertainty of this approach, and as a result, we discovered the potential and possibility that was available for her. She found another new mother to interact with and saw how she could reach out to others for support. As a true leader, I was no longer needed on a regular basis in her life. I had worked my way out of a job, which, for me, was a sign of success.

Over the years as a nurse and a helper, I had learned to be really good at seeing the problems in life. In many cases, I thought I had the perfect solution too.

Often, though, others didn't appreciate my help. Maybe they didn't see the situation as a problem. Maybe they were triggered by my solutions. If I came across as the expert who could solve their problems, they'd get defensive, thinking I saw them as inadequate. Once I started looking for gifts instead, I saw how those gifts could be the answer they were looking for.

When my husband was at a crossroads in his work and looking for a new job, it would have been easy to focus on the problem: no job. Instead, we talked about what things he enjoys doing, what he is good at, what brings him joy. He is creative and artistic, a skilled woodworker and furniture designer. These gifts led him to start his own business of making furniture and designing new spaces for renovation projects.

This change didn't happen quickly for me. Years of problem-solving kept me locked in the old way of being. However, I kept going on the trail of becoming a true leader and made a conscious choice to focus on the gifts I saw in others as opposed to thinking I had all the answers. Each day, I looked for the gifts in my world and in the people I interacted with. With time, I saw the positive impact of this way of being, and it became an integral aspect of how I showed up as a true leader.

Face Fear

I was preparing a speech in preparation for an upcoming retreat. Not just any speech, but a presentation to inspire my listeners to create change in their lives as they heard my story. I was crafting a talk that would describe a challenge I'd overcome and, in the process, offer the possibility of transformation to my audience. I was inspired to show up as a true leader, sharing from my own wisdom rather than paraphrasing what I thought the experts might say.

As it turned out, writing the speech was the easy part. There would also be the video of me giving the talk, which would be sent off to the conference organizers for feedback. I cringed at this idea! I felt stuck, paralyzed with fear.

My inner critic argued loudly with me, "Are you serious? Marjorie on video for others to watch?"

It was a huge step of vulnerability for me, someone who didn't even like taking selfies. Seeing myself on the screen was not easy. I found myself feeling embarrassed, shy, and critical of how I looked and sounded. Deep down, I also knew that my quest to show up as a true leader meant being willing to be seen, just as I am, imperfections and all.

I sent off the first draft with a sense of impending doom. Then I got the feedback. I was encouraged to be more authentic. I rolled my eyes and thought, I knew I wasn't any good at this. How could I be "myself" on video?

In the midst of this, I shared it with my coach. She wondered, "What would your Wise Woman have to offer you right now?"

I had forgotten to pay attention to her and hadn't been listening to her whispers. But she was there all the time.

My Wise Woman spoke softly and reminded me to slow down. Her voice had been drowned out by the distractions in my life: the well-meaning advice of others, the comparison game when I saw the videos of other speakers, the frenzied pace to complete the speech on time. I stopped and was quiet, a silence that created space for wisdom. Wisdom can't catch up with me if I'm speeding along the path trying to outrun fear.

LEADERSHIP

I had a deadline to meet, and I was rushing to complete the task. I didn't have time to stop and listen. When fear is in control, I feel a push to keep going at all costs. What if I get too far behind? I'm desperate to keep up, and the idea of slowing down just brings up more fear that I'll never get it done.

So I trusted my Wise Woman's advice and took a break. I rested. I went for a long walk by the ocean. I took time to practice my gestures and expressions. Instead of pushing myself to finish, I trusted it would get done on time. I talked to my fear and told it to relax and keep quiet. I knew it was ready to shout in my ear at a moment's notice, but, rather than ignoring it, I set boundaries for how it could relate to me. I was reminded of the way I interact with my inner critic. The counter-intuitive approach of making friends with fear worked for me.

My Wise Woman had another piece of advice—step back. Take a moment to look at the big picture. Yes, the details are important and, yes, little things matter. Significance resides in the small pieces of the puzzle. The thing is, I was getting bogged down by the details.

The big question for me was: Why am I doing this? What's my motivation? In five years, would this matter? Will the anxiety I feel today seem as important then? Where do I want to focus my energy? What might shift as I widen my view of this project?

My perspective changed as I stepped back and viewed my speech with a wide-angle lens.

I realized I wanted to inspire my listeners and share my insights. I was excited to have them hear what I was learning. My nervousness and worry about how I looked in the video lessened as I focused on my big why. I reminded myself of my passion to share my story as a true leader with wisdom to impart. I breathed deeply and looked at what I'd already completed. I brought myself back to the present moment rather than the unknown future. Fear took a back seat.

As I practiced presence and silence, I found riches awaiting me. I asked my inner wisdom, "What is possible?" I imagined what I was longing for. In this case, I wanted to be a speaker who could capture the audience's attention with the first word and keep them sitting at the edge of their seats until I finished to a standing ovation. Even though my dreams seemed impossible, I knew they were the first step to completing a powerful speech.

My bigger longing was to show up as a true leader in all areas of my life. My fear of looking awkward and foolish was keeping me from stepping forward with power. I wanted to let go of my worry about not getting it right and lead from my deep knowing.

As I listened to my inner wisdom, I gained confidence in following its nudges and whispers. I experienced ease and flow as I prepared my speech. I trusted my judgment as to how I would speak. I let go of pleasing and comparing myself to others. I began to see the positive effects of being myself. I felt relaxed and happy as I practiced, experimenting with facial expressions and tone of voice that felt natural to me. I found it easier to remember the words and eventually put my notes aside. A coaching colleague offered to record my final draft, and I found playfulness and fun in creating with her.

Fear didn't leave me completely that day. I continue to face my fear and remind it that I am in charge. I tell my fear I have the resources to support myself through my dark times and to stay behind me on this trail to being a true leader. As I connect with my inner wisdom, I am able to move forward with lightness and joy. Despite its presence, fear no longer keeps me from moving toward my dreams.

Be Strong and Fierce

It was time for me to go. I was heading to the retreat hosted by the leader of the coaching program I had been part of for the past eight months. The retreat would include opportunities to learn, connect, and play with my coaching colleagues from all over the world as well as give the speech I had been preparing for the past few weeks. I loved writing, but the idea of speaking was another thing altogether. This was a totally different experience from the speaking I did as a workshop facilitator, where the content I spoke about was based on the teachings of others. This speech was written from my heart and told my personal story.

I'd been practicing and longed to show up strong and powerful as I spoke. I worried my mind would go blank, that I would stand on the stage feeling foolish with nothing to say. At the same time, I wanted to prove I could do it. Saying yes to giving this speech was the mark of a true leader, stepping into my power.

I also knew that being strong included caring for myself and being willing to receive from the other women. I set the intention to be curious and learn what being strong meant to them. Strength is embedded in community, and I wanted to experience the richness of how partnerships can lead to a renewed belief in my own power.

In the weeks leading up to the retreat, I set some intentions for how I wanted to show up. I knew that I would be the oldest participant there. I wanted to be both a wise elder, who would inspire the younger women, as well as like a kid again, unlimited by age. I wanted to be powerful and free as I gave my speech and let go of the expectations of how it might be received. I wanted to trust that my listeners would get what was perfect for them.

My freshwater pearl bracelet glistened on my wrist and reminded me of my strength and power as a woman with the gifts to share her story in a meaningful and inviting way. It was my symbol of my intention coming true. Full of courage and confidence, I brought my full self to my presentation.

I took the stage and stood tall in front of the group of women, relaxed and smiling. I envisioned myself as stately and beautiful as I took a deep breath and began to speak. My opening line was captivating and grabbed the listeners' attention. I had a sense of play, authenticity, and vulnerability. I found my light-hearted, joyful approach fun and inspiring, and the audience's response told me they were also inspired. They applauded enthusiastically and cheered. A listener commented that the light in the room loved the soul behind my eyes. She saw my intention to be a vessel of love and receive love back from each woman there.

I know that being strong and fierce in my power means taking responsibility for my own experience. After this experience, I saw myself as a true leader, strong and powerful as I trusted my inner wisdom and moved forward despite my fear, showing up with an emphatic yes to my dreams. This belief in myself would also support me in saying no when I needed to set boundaries. I am a true leader who can make choices that are aligned with inner wisdom.

Set Boundaries

Walking into the unit, I stopped short. What was all that? Through the glass walls of my office, all I could see were boxes. Piles of them, big and small, stacked all around my desk and overflowing into the corners of the room.

It would be a full, busy day in the operating room of the Abbotsford Community Hospital. I was head nurse of the recovery room where patients woke up from anaesthesia before transfer back to the surgical ward. I enjoyed the leadership and sense of adventure as each day brought a fresh slate of patients. At the same time, I felt insecure. I'd recently been promoted to this position.

I really wanted to be a successful leader, which I thought of as being competent, easy-going, and fun to work with. It was challenging for me to move from the role of staff nurse to managing nurses who had been my colleagues. I was still figuring out what that looked like.

I looked at the boxes again and shook my head not knowing what was going on. Then I heard the news. One of the nurses was moving and wanted a place to store her boxes overnight. She'd put them in my office without bothering to ask my permission. I could hardly walk to my desk and there was no room for anyone else to sit in my office. I chose not to say anything, telling myself it was a nuisance I could manage. I moved a few boxes around and managed to find room for my desk chair.

Then a longtime friend and colleague asked, "What's with all the boxes, Marjorie?" I explained it had been done without my permission, and she told me, "You don't have to let people take advantage of you like that, you know."

Wow, was that what I was doing? I thought I was being flexible and thoughtful. I wanted to be easy to get along with, someone who didn't get upset too easily. I wanted the staff to like me and accept me as the new leader in the unit.

As I paid attention to my experience, I noticed how messy and cluttered my office was. I felt stressed and anxious as I sat there surrounded by boxes. My shoulders felt tight and my face flushed. My jaw was clenched and my breathing was shallow. I asked myself, "Why are these here at all? Why choose my office for them? This is my personal space and whoever did this had no right to use it as a storage locker, especially without my permission!" I wanted to stand up for myself and get the boxes out of my space.

Distracted and upset, I knew I was in no condition to start the workday. I wouldn't have the focus necessary to be an effective leader. But I was the only one who could control my experience. I had a choice to make.

What does it mean to be a true leader in a case like this?

After taking a few deep breaths, I reminded myself that I was an important part of the team and required an office where I could concentrate and focus on my job. My role was to support nurses in providing safe patient care. If I was to show up as a true leader, I had to demonstrate that

LEADERSHIP

I valued myself and saw myself as worthy of respect. My office space was my domain and should be off-limits to others. I had to speak up to show up as a true leader.

Once I showed up in this way, I was able to let go of my resentment and shift my focus toward the duties of the day. I proved I could speak up for myself and say no when necessary even when I wasn't sure of the reception I'd get. I had placed my self-worth ahead of my desire to be liked. I gained confidence in myself as I knew I could check in with my body's signals and then listen to my inner wisdom to move forward with integrity. Setting boundaries is an integral part of being a true leader.

Setting boundaries in my personal life can be even more challenging than with work colleagues. When my children were young, I would often find myself picking up after them or making lunches. It took some time, but eventually, I chose to delegate, and they learned to do many things for themselves. Now it is time for me to set boundaries around caring for my grandchildren. As much as I love spending time with them, I do have my own schedule to consider before I unthinkingly say yes to requests for childcare. I am learning to set boundaries for myself, too. I love spending time with friends, and there are times when I say yes too quickly to a coffee date or lunch party. Then I wonder why I am so exhausted and have no energy for doing things I want to accomplish for myself.

Practicing *no* leads to a freedom to give what I call a full-bodied *yes* when the whole body vibrates in accord. Sometimes my full-bodied yes is peaceful, possessed by calm energy, free from tension or tightness, relaxed and contented with the steps ahead. Sometimes it is excited, characterized by a huge smile, arms held wide open. I may feel like dancing or jumping up and down as I lean forward to declare: "Let's get going!"

As I've learned, in order for my *yes* to be authentic, my *no* must also be. When I say yes but mean no, my health is directly impacted. Repeated acts of inauthenticity have left me with a dysfunctional thyroid, the gland that symbolizes speaking up for myself. Of course! It makes sense that this part of my body would cry out for help, and it took a combination of supplements and coaching for me to regain my health. My thyroid has become an early warning system for me, and I have my levels checked regularly. When they're irregular, I check in with myself: How am I doing with setting boundaries? It may be a signal for me to sharpen my saying-no skills.

With a full-bodied yes, I'm fully ready to do what's asked of me, the tension of doing one thing and wanting to do another no longer part of the experience. I give myself time to think about what I want to do and know I can say no if I want to. I say yes because I choose to, not to please others or avoid conflict.

When I say yes from this place, I feel energized, light-hearted, and have more respect for myself. No longer in victim mode, complaining and filled with self-pity, I'm more myself. When I set boundaries, I model true leadership and encourage others to do the same. It's a ripple effect of lessened confusion and resentment and increased ease and flow.

The viewpoint from this spot on the trail is breathtaking as I celebrate the steps I've taken to get here. Gazing over the valley below, I see the beauty in my relationships with my family, who no longer second-guess my response when they request my help with childcare, knowing I respond honestly. I catch a glimpse of myself from this vantage point and see a woman who is comfortable in her own skin, who values herself and is her own advocate. I'm proud of how she takes risks to say no and let go of what others might think of her. She has courage and faith in her own wisdom. As a true leader, I am committed to being authentic with my boundaries and experience the power of yes and no.

Stay Committed

The wind whipped my face and the rain fell relentlessly. I picked up my pace hoping to outrun the wet and cold. I was training for a marathon, and this was my endurance-building day. My legs were heavy and my lungs burned. I asked myself, "How much farther?"

I kept going, shouting encouragement to my running buddies. They cheered me on, and I felt less alone. Instead of focusing on my cold hands and wet feet, I imagined crossing the finish line and having the medal placed around my neck. This was my first marathon attempt and I could almost taste the feeling of euphoria and hear the words of congratulation. I wanted that medal, and I wasn't going to give up—no matter how messy it felt.

Part of my dream of completing the Vancouver Marathon was committing to putting in the training hours. I knew I'd only be prepared if I put the hours in, no matter the weather. Sure, some days I wondered if it was worth it, tempted to skip a training run or workout. Who would really notice? I reminded myself that *I* would notice. I was doing this for me, not for anyone else. My commitment was to my dream, and I was determined to keep going.

Training included rest days and a commitment to my nutrition. I chose to eat wisely and made sure I took days off to prevent injury and burnout. Having a healthy meal and going to bed early on a Saturday night was never easy, but I learned the hard way that it made me much stronger and more energetic for the next day's run of twenty miles or more.

I couldn't have done it without support. My husband understood the rigorous training schedule and adapted to a new routine when I was gone for long periods. It required some planning with our extended family and wasn't always easy to plan events, but they graciously accepted that I needed to put in the hours, and we were still able to have family time. They were curious about how I was doing, and deep down I knew they were proud of me for taking on this challenge in spite of the complications involved.

I wanted to have a sense of partnership—rather than competition—with my running buddies, counting on them for support as well. I wanted all those miles together to be enjoyable. This included them seeing me as I really was, which required my willingness to inform them if I was discouraged or wanted to quit. I asked them to cheer me on and let me know how they were doing. I found a place of acceptance and belonging as I was open, honest, and listened to their experiences.

I hardly slept a wink the night before the marathon. Getting dressed, I wondered what I'd been thinking about when I signed up for this race. My stomach was in knots and my legs were shaking as I approached the start line. It seemed like an impossible goal for me to attempt.

Then I met up with my running friends and something changed as we encouraged each other before the race. I wasn't the only one who was nervous, and we laughed our anxiety off together.

LEADERSHIP

Then I heard it. The starting gun had sounded. We were off!

There was a rush of excitement as I ran with the huge crowd. I'd never run with so many people at once. I loved being part of the energy surrounding me. I was running my first marathon, and I was excited and proud.

The reality soon set in. I was on my own in the midst of hundreds of runners. Running was a solitary experience, and I knew it was up to me to keep going. My pace was slow and steady. I didn't even try to keep up with my training partners. I listened to my body, and I knew what would work best for me. I kept to my plan—run for ten minutes, walk for one. I focused on breathing and drinking water. The scenery was breathtaking as we ran between the ocean and the distant mountains. The crowd cheered us on. I felt strong and powerful.

Twenty-six miles is a long distance to run, and by mile seventeen, I thought I was done. How could I continue? But my training supported me, and I said to myself, "This is just another long run on a Sunday morning at home." I cheered myself on with the reminder I was strong and capable of finishing. One step after the other, again and again. I ate energy bars and kept going. I had no sign of injuries, but I was weary.

At one point, I saw my husband cheering me on, camera in hand. I slowed down to wave, a big smile on my face. "See you at the finish line," I called out and kept running. The last mile was a mix of emotions. I was exhausted and excited. I knew a group of family and friends awaited me at the end. I was getting there, determined to have that medal placed around my neck. The thought of this kept me going.

The long hours of training were worth it. I crossed the finish line and was overcome with tears of joy and pride. I found a spot where I could be alone, breathing in the reality of what I had accomplished. The medal was around my neck. I knew I was done, but I could scarcely believe it. I had dreamt of this moment for so long. I was now a marathon runner. I had been determined and committed, and I was successful. I wanted to soak in every sensation, every emotion. I knew how significant this was for me as a symbol of my strength and power as a woman.

After my time alone, I found my cheerleaders. My husband, children, and friends greeted me with big hugs, flowers, and plans for a party.

The celebration that followed was full of foot massages, cold drinks, and yummy food, all of which I gratefully received. I listened to the lively sounds of music and conversation with a deep sense of satisfaction and contentment.

For years I had longed to join the marathon group at the Running Room where I trained, and now I was part of an elite group of people who had actually completed a marathon. I saw myself differently. It was a special feeling for me. I was a woman who kept her word, proud of my devotion to reaching my goal. Even when I was tempted to quit, my integrity and persistence kept me going. I felt the magic of fulfilling my dream! I knew that this experience would inspire me for the rest of my life. If I could do this, what else could I accomplish? Running a marathon was a metaphor for taking on challenges to come. I felt confident and empowered as I looked at the medal in my hands.

I've since completed many more races. Despite the tediousness of long training runs and anxiousness I feel at the start line, the camaraderie has nourished my soul and kept me going, the marathons themselves becoming a symbol of commitment, adventure, and friendship.

LEADERSHIP

My husband built me a beautiful shadow box to display my medals. As I look at them, I'm reminded of what is possible when I set a goal for myself. They inspired me as I set out to write my book, noticing the similarities between this and the experience of training for a marathon.

Commitment is a sign that I'm not doing something to please others. If I'm not fully committed to my vision, it's unlikely to happen. Running can be a lonely activity. Even when in a group, the running is still up to me. Writing is even more so. I may share my ideas with others, but it's up to me to sit down and put those ideas into words. I can't depend on others to keep me motivated.

Completing a goal means I keep going even when I don't feel like it. How does this relate to listening to my body and taking a break when my body's exhausted and my spirits are low? This is the mystery of what it means to be committed. It's a paradox each of us must explore for ourselves.

Training for marathons, I struggled with the dance between the pressure to keep going at all costs and the flow of paying attention to my body's messages. I took time off if I was injured or sick, knowing my body would take longer to heal if I ran in that condition. A rainy day, though, was no excuse not to run. I got proper rain gear and grew accustomed to getting wet even though it wasn't always easy.

I remember waking up early one morning to rain pounding against my bedroom window. I was so tempted to stay warm and dry in bed; running in the rain was the last thing I wanted to do. Then I reminded myself why I was training. I reaffirmed my commitment, got out of bed, and headed to the Running Club.

On this trail called commitment, I'm clear on what my goal is. It's not just a passing thought, but one I'm really excited about, and I take actions that support me in reaching it.

This is true for me also in writing. Writing my book, imagining seeing it in print and signing it for my readers, hearing how touched and inspired they are, I would get butterflies in my stomach. I wrote this book in the hot days of summer that called for play and fun outside. I struggled with staying committed when I was invited to the beach or for a picnic at the park. When I chose to say no in order to get a chapter written, I renewed my vow to myself and my vision of completing my book.

I love the outdoors, and while writing a book over the summer brought challenges I hadn't expected, I looked at the ways to make the most of it. I wrote in my front courtyard where the visits of the hummingbirds and the sound of the water fountain kept me company. The shade of the maple tree beat air conditioning any day, and the fragrance of the sweet peas was pure inspiration.

I learned to pace myself as I wrote, taking rest days as I did in marathon training. Sometimes I needed reminding. In the midst of the first round of revising my manuscript, I became irritable and weepy at the slightest provocation. My husband asked me if I'd taken any recent breaks. His comment only added to my impatient mood. I had a deadline, I still had work to do. The revisions were taking much longer than anticipated. How could I stop now?

For a day or so, I was in a dark place of shame and discouragement. One afternoon, I couldn't concentrate. Feeling hopeless, I stretched out on my bed. I heard my Wise Woman whisper softly, "Is this the lightness you want in your life as you write this book?" I breathed deeply and accepted that I needed a break. I wanted to write with ease and flow. I took four days to play and spend time with my family, and as a result, I regained my energy for the revisions that remained.

Life is not an interruption to my writing. Life is what my book is about. I trusted that time spent caring for my grandchildren would rejuvenate me. I was inspired by their playful energy and willingness to go bike riding with me. I took time to weed the flower bed, feeling calm and grounded as I dug in the dirt. My life's activities added to my creativity, and I learned to pay attention to my body and its needs on this path to writing a book.

Commitment isn't for the faint of heart. It takes courage and stamina, perseverance and persistence. I show up as a true leader as I pay attention to what's best for me and follow through on my promises to myself. When I say I'll do something and then do it, I'm keeping my word to myself and living with integrity. Even when my commitment requires a break, this isn't a time for shame. Instead, I acknowledge my actions and choose to keep going. Sometimes a break is needed from the rigours of a gruelling schedule. When I accept this, I come back with renewed energy.

Commitment shifts and fluctuates. The mark of a true leader is the willingness to accept what life brings, acknowledge the messiness, and trust that whatever happens will work out for the best. In spite of commitment and desire, there may be times when I'm unable to fulfill my vision. Rather than seeing this as a failure, I take a different approach by focusing on what I have control over and accepting what I can't change. Flexibility in the twists and turns on the path to commitment is a key component to living the life of a true leader.

As I became more settled in myself, I showed up, and they loved me.

TRUE BELONGING

>>>———▶

The kitchen table had been moved into the living room. This was a special occasion.

My friends and I sat in our chairs looking at the festive tablecloth and delicious food. Peanut butter and banana sandwiches, juice, presents waiting to be unwrapped.... Such simple fare, and yet I felt rich as a queen. It was my ninth birthday, and I was having a party.

This was a time just for me. My little brothers and sisters weren't invited, and I felt so lucky to be with my friends.

One present was a book. Another was an apron that my friend's mother had sewn for me out of a terry towel. Then there was the banana birthday cake, gooey and moist, with clouds of brown sugar frosting.

But what I remember most isn't the food or the presents. In the midst of our conversation, I said something and everyone laughed with delight. They laughed with me, enjoying my sense of humour.

I was astonished, thinking, wow, my friends really like me! They think I'm fun to be with! I'm important to them. I didn't have to accomplish anything to get my friends' approval. It didn't matter that the furniture was well-used or that the food was simple. Our friendship transcended any differences in our financial or social status. They saw and witnessed me. I was noticed and appreciated for who I was. I showed up, and they loved me.

In my large family, I had often felt invisible. Six children, aged nine years to six months, meant there was a lot of competing for attention from our parents. I only seemed to get noticed when I helped with chores or childcare. At my birthday party, I was the centre of attention. I belonged. I loved the feeling.

Friendship seems to get more tricky as time goes by. I know there are "seasons" of friendship, and I also know that it's challenging to leave a relationship when it's no longer life-giving.

After my coach had introduced me to my Wise Woman and the first Emerging Women conference had opened my eyes to my potential as a woman of wisdom and powerful feminine energy, I excitedly came home one evening and told my longtime friends about my insights. I didn't get the response I had expected. Where was their excitement in my new knowledge? They didn't seem interested in or curious about what I had to say. I struggled to no avail to describe what had occurred. I felt frustrated, as if I was speaking a different language.

I thought back to how I had been as a young girl, always trying to please others and following what the experts told me. At this point in my life, I yearned to be authentic and lead from my own wisdom. Here I was, passionately trying to communicate what my heart was telling me, and no one seemed to understand how important it was. Was I on the wrong path? Should I go back to how I had been?

This was the start of a lonely time for me. There were days when I wondered if I was making a difference in the world at all. I didn't hear many positive comments from others. I felt sad and discouraged. My conference companions were scattered all over the world. Keeping in touch over email and video calls wasn't the same as meeting with like-minded women in person. I continued to meet with my former friends and continued to notice the disconnect between my values and their interests. They weren't wrong, and neither was I. There was just a gap between us. I felt the loss of my connection with them and, at the same time, didn't want to lose what I had learned.

At times, I wondered if I'd ever emerge from the dark, overgrown forest to a glimmer of light. I hadn't expected the shadows to be such a big part of this stage of the journey. I struggled with impatience, doubting myself and my ability to keep going. I'm so grateful to Alison and her way of witnessing me during this time. I could hardly wait for our coaching sessions when she reminded me to stop, take a deep breath, and connect to my Wise Woman.

I wouldn't give up what I now knew to be true. I trusted myself and believed in what I was sharing. I wanted to focus on learning more about my inner wisdom and the gifts that would lead others to find joy in their lives.

Many of my own gifts have emerged in the years since the conference. Instead of blindly following the experts, I seek out mentors and guides. I follow their suggestions with discernment. I now know to trust myself, accept uncertainty, and be a true leader. I no longer push through at all costs to get things done. I have compassion for myself, focusing on play and pleasure as a way to live authentically.

I continued to write about what was happening to me. I discovered podcasts and books that resonated with and inspired me. I played with the idea that I could be my own friend. I became more comfortable with solitude and planned days to be on my own. Walking in the forest or by the ocean was a time of reflection and renewal for me. I witnessed my life journey and celebrated the wisdom I accessed by listening to my Wise Woman.

There are times when I slip back into my usual patterns of blame and judgment. I was invited to a luncheon with a group of women and imagined it would be a time of connection. Within an hour, I was restless and wanted to go home. I felt impatient with the topics that seemed to interest everyone else.

I said my goodbyes and drove home with a mix of emotions, among them emptiness and sadness that the conversation hadn't been enriching. Angry and frustrated, I wondered what was wrong with me that I couldn't fit in and just enjoy the lunch like everyone else. Then I got anxious. Would I ever find a group of friends where I belonged?

I stewed and fumed for the afternoon, trying to distract myself with things around the house. Exhausted, I gave up forcing myself to be productive. Instead I took a hot bubble bath. As I soaked in the tub, I heard my Wise Woman. She reminded me about accepting myself as I am, even if all my stuff is not figured out, loving myself even in the mess and mire of shame. I realized I was so drained energetically because I wasn't being authentic. I had fallen into the old pattern of trying to please others by going to the lunch when what I really wanted was to stay home and focus on what lights me up.

Life seemed shaky and nothing seemed to be working out the way I wanted it to. I took comfort in Pema Chodron's words from her book *When Things Fall Apart*, "Groundlessness ... is the kind of testing that spiritual warriors need in order to awaken their hearts." I made room in my heart for uncertainty, remembering that disappointment is not necessarily the end of the trail. Perhaps a wonderful adventure was around the next bend.

The next day I gently placed my story into the loving arms of a dear soul sister. We had booked a call several days earlier and—of course—it was exactly the right time for me to meet with her. With her support, I was reminded of how crucial it is for me to be myself, which gave me freedom to admit what interactions I want and give myself permission to follow my desires. There was nothing wrong with me leaving the lunch early to do what I wanted.

I took the opportunity to practice self-compassion, letting go of shaming myself and accepting that I was on a journey that could not be rushed. It takes time to shift my pattern away from looking to others for belonging. Speaking kindly to myself, I came to a place of calm and self-acceptance.

As I became more settled in myself, I found women I related to and shared a language with. I shared my longing for "soul" connection and was invited to join them in a Women's Circle. I noticed that as I let go of needing acknowledgment from others and showered love upon myself, I was seen and appreciated by the people I interacted with. Or was it that I now saw the gifts they offered me? My heart was open to receiving from others as I received from myself. Letting go allowed abundance to flow into my life.

I attended the second annual Emerging Women Conference. As I met women from the year before and made new friends, I immediately felt at home. I could be myself without worrying about being misunderstood. There was an ease and flow to my relationships. This was my community, and I embraced the joy waiting for me.

As these women witnessed me, they honoured me for my life experiences and the gifts I brought them. They thanked me for my words of wisdom and asked me for advice about life's challenges. I saw myself as the true leader I was, stepping into my eldership and celebrating my age rather than hiding the fact that I was a grandmother and much older than most of them.

I'm aware of how important it was for me to authentically receive from the women who witnessed me, which, upon reflection, has happened many other times in my life.

I think of my critical care co-workers affirming me as a calm presence during a crisis. They told me they depended on my clear directions and quick-thinking. Their comments helped me see myself as a competent nurse and a strong leader. It's true: even when I was shaking, nervous about the next steps, I stayed focused and did what needed to be done.

I had a long and disappointing time of it when I wanted to move from staff nurse in public health nursing to a different role. After many unsuccessful interviews, I finally got the exact job I wanted as workshop facilitator. A colleague told me she was struck by my integrity during this frustrating process. She saw me continuing to be professional and work hard even though I wanted a change. I was touched by her words and saw myself as a woman who follows through on responsibility even when discontented in my current position.

I've been encouraged by the comments of workshop participants in classes I've taught. They said, "Your stories help me understand concepts" or "You model what you teach. You're willing to admit when you say something hurtful or may have offended someone" or "You walk your talk." I saw myself as a mentor and guide with the gifts of teaching in a clear and communicative way.

There's a connection between being seen by others and my ability to believe what they say and receive it graciously. As a true leader, I model the importance of receiving. I am the "Queen of Receiving," not a princess who requires being cared for. I am Queen Marjorie who receives graciously and humbly. Unless I love myself, I'm unable to participate in the gift exchange that is receiving love from others.

This way of receiving transforms my relationships, creating a flow of giving and receiving that is itself creative and community-building. I no longer brush off compliments or downplay accomplishments. I now see how doing so diminishes the compliment giver, robbing us both of joy.

There is a delicate balance between my ability to affirm myself and accepting affirmation from others. This means that even before others tell me how they see me, I'm able to see myself. Think back to the pancake breakfast at that cafe. Part of me saw myself as a loving mother, so I was able to receive a compliment from a stranger, and her acknowledgement, in turn, allowed me to see myself more fully, reminding me of my loving mother qualities.

I benefit from being witnessed, and the person seeing me is impacted by my response. A life-giving connection happens as we engage in the gift exchange, which lends our lives an energy of love and lightness. The ripples continue as we are then on the lookout for gifts in others' lives and as we, in turn, tell others how we see them and what we appreciate.

From the personal work I have done, I know my personality is the type that thrives on being seen. When I am noticed, I experience it as being loved. When I think I'm being disregarded or ignored, I jump to the conclusion that I'm unimportant or, worse, unloved. This is a slippery path into the swamp of self-pity where I blame others for my suffering. When I'm waiting for a return call or email, it seems to take forever. I often focus on my feelings of rejection rather than the possibility that the other person may have a hectic life and will get back to me when possible. It's another step for me to navigate in the dance of seeing myself and being seen by others.

Even though I have a longing to feel connected and have people in my life who witness me, I'm learning I can meet those needs for myself. I can be my own cheerleader and affirm myself. I no longer need others' approval or recognition to feel content. With practice, I've been able to let go of what others do or don't say to me. As I do that, I'm better able to hear the whispers in my heart. My inner wisdom speaks to me, and I'm comforted to know that I belong to the wide circle of human beings all over the world who are love. I am connected because I am following my heart and learning to trust myself. I no longer feel desperate when I have a day without a coffee date. I let go of my annoyance when a friend takes several days to answer my email.

On this journey, I grew aware of the difference between loneliness and solitude. Being on my own doesn't mean I have to be lonely. The quietness of solitude has, in fact, led me to deepen my relationship with myself. What a beautiful realization to have. I now feel at peace even when I'm not with trusted friends, knowing that, when the time is right, we will connect. I trust in the deep bonds of love that keep us together even when we aren't together in person.

Today I celebrate the love I have for myself and the trust I have that I belong regardless of how others respond to me. I'm seeing how it's possible to enjoy my own company. I love the gifts I get from others while, at the same time, knowing I can name my own gifts and be proud of myself for who I am. Trusting myself is a worthwhile action, and the love I have for myself bubbles over to touch the people who surround me.

This is the birthplace of sharing my gifts with others. As I wrote my book, I saw myself as a conduit for wisdom and love. I have a story that's bigger than I am. I've been given the gift of writing, and this book has become my offering to the world. I was called to write it. I answered the call to use my gifts, and, as I accept the call, I put on the shawl my coach, Alison, gave me for my birthday one year. It symbolized the presence of my Wise Woman, reminding me that my love for myself is strong protection against the critical comments that are sure to come. They can't stop or harm me.

I open my heart to my inner wisdom and keep my soul soft and inviting in order to experience what I needed to go through to be a clear, open channel.

Epilogue:

A LOVE LETTER FROM MY WISE WOMAN

>>>———▶

My Dear Marjorie,

What a journey this has been! Hiking together with you has been an adventure like no other. As we reach this resting place, I want to celebrate what has happened. Let's take some time to breathe, reflect, and enjoy the view.

What did you know about trusting yourself before we started? It seemed as though you were so used to depending on others for guidance that you didn't even know you could check in with yourself. I want to say how thrilled I am that you now know to listen to your intuition and trust your inner wisdom. I'm always here to hold you, listen to you, and guide you as you stop and listen to my quiet whisper deep down in your soul.

Your inner critic has been hiking along with us, and I am proud of how you've made friends with her. She has no power over you because you take the time to listen to her and then tell her that all will be well, even if you don't follow her advice. You were clear with her when you told her she could walk on the same path with you only if she kept quiet and followed your lead. She was not the one to call time for a rest break or a snack, as she typically does so out of fear. That is your job, Marjorie, and I see you doing that from a place of love for yourself. Way to go!

Receiving was such an important lesson on this journey we travelled together. In the past, you tended to brush off a compliment about your appearance or your abilities. I remember you shrugging your shoulder and saying, "Oh, really?" Or you might say, "I was just lucky I had a good day teaching today."

As you started understanding the importance of the gift exchange, you learned how to receive. You now know that it is a gift to the person complimenting you when you offer gracious thanks in return. No excuses or minimizing what you actually accomplished. I now see you as a woman who is wise in the ways of receiving all that life has to offer you.

You have learned to see gifts everywhere around you. It is a delight for me to see you expecting magic and then receiving with an open heart. I celebrate you taking a leap and trusting that your needs will be supplied. All those times when this occurred are evidence of the abundance that keeps showing up along the way. I'm glad you took the risk to follow a trail that looked steep and challenging. The spectacular view made it all worthwhile.

Taking responsibility and practicing clear communication was a winding and challenging path, wasn't it? It's so easy to blame others for your problems. I saw you swallowing your pride and looking at what your part was in a relationship breakdown. You navigated the obstacles and overcame your assumptions about what was going on. As a result, you were able to clear up hurt feelings and move on in partnership with the people in your life. This is a major life lesson!

I wondered at times if we would ever make it through the trail of uncertainty. There were so many switch backs, dead ends, and steep climbs. And, yet, here we are. We did it! One thing that helped was your attitude of awaiting unexpected gifts. When you reminded yourself that whatever happens is a gift, your attitude shifted. You became more aware of the present moment, and you saw the benefit in what might have seemed like a huge problem. People showed up along the way with encouraging words that helped you see yourself differently. You received the affirmations and became powerful and confident. You have a beautiful way of gathering community around you, and, because of this, you and they benefit. Life becomes more fun and no one is left to struggle and strive alone.

You've also seen the power of looking for the gifts in others. You have been a sleuth for the goodness all around you, and you have found it. The gifts you have in your life have also been a way of overcoming roadblocks on the trail. This way of living leads to lightness and joy rather than discouragement and depression caused by life's problems.

I saw you struggle with surrender. You fought against what didn't please you, and it took a long time for you to discover the trail of acceptance. After a few falls and scrapes, you realized that focusing your energy on what you have control over is the best way to go. Worry and anxiety have decreased since you started living from this space.

My dearest Marjorie, I am especially excited to see how you have learned to live authentically by putting yourself first. When we started this journey, you were such a helper and always seemed to think of others before considering your needs. You thought this was the way to gain approval and how you lived your life for many years. This led to ill health, resentment, and a feeling of never being enough.

What a beautiful transformation I see in you! You now pay attention to what your body is telling you and what it needs to stay healthy and happy. This means you are willing to say what you want and go for it without apology. Of course, then you have more to give others from your overflowing cup of joy and love.

There has been a major shift in how you feel your feelings. You know that allowing emotions such as sadness, anger, and fear to flow through you is the path to health and vitality. Instead of pushing your emotions down and pretending everything is okay, you express your emotions and feel them deeply. You cry, you vent your anger, and you admit when you are afraid, both to yourself and to trusted friends. What is especially beautiful to see is how this translates into you caring for yourself. Self-compassion is your new normal, and, as you show love to yourself, you have a gracious and inviting energy that draws others to you.

Exploring play and pleasure was one of my favourite paths. When you discovered the secret that life becomes filled with lightness when you follow your pleasure, I was brimming over with laughter and delight. I also saw how others wanted what you had. It was so obvious how your energy was coming from a place of deep pleasure and joy and how effortless things became for you. This is cause for a party! So much of your life used to be about getting it right, pleasing others, and being a helper. Isn't it just delicious to see how you are getting it right, pleasing others, and helping them by following your desires and making pleasure and play a priority? It's no surprise to me that this is the way life is unfolding for you.

You have always been a leader. As a young girl, your classmates looked up to you. You naturally took charge and led the way in projects, group games, and planning events. All the while, you made sure you pleased those you viewed as the authority figures in your life. You led in ways that would make them happy.

I saw you transform your style of leadership as we hiked along. You no longer lead in order to meet the expectations of others. You lead from your inner wisdom and what your soul tells you to do. You do this even if it seems to be against the norm or others don't understand. You lead in ways that support your values regardless of whether anyone else is following.

This is "true leadership."

You've encountered obstacles along the trail that have taken persistence to overcome. There was that big boulder of fear. You knew it was pointless to ignore it. It wasn't going to go away, so you faced it with courage. You listened to what its message was for you rather than ignoring it or pushing it aside. After you heard it wanted to keep you safe, you were able to step into your leadership and remind fear that you already are safe. You're doing just fine without needing to follow its advice. You have supports and tools that you know can protect you. You have loved ones in your life to call on, and you trust that all will be well. You no longer give fear any power.

I celebrate how you are showing up in your fierce and powerful energy. Look at you!

One of the things I love about you is your desire to show love to others. You are kind and helpful, quick to respond to requests for help. However, I saw the shadow side of this in your life as we kept trekking along. There were times when you were already exhausted but kept on giving. I saw your resentment and weariness, and I knew you had some important lessons to learn about saying no when you really meant no. You came to realize that saying yes when you are depleted isn't truly loving at all. It's more important to be honest and say what you are capable of. Instead of saying yes immediately, you've started saying, "Let me get back to you." Then, you check in with your intuition and see if you should agree. You model true leadership by being authentic and saying what's best for you. The beautiful thing is that others prefer this and are inspired by your way of being clear and setting boundaries.

Then there is the practice of commitment and discipline. You have moved from pushing yourself at all costs to paying attention to your body's needs and taking breaks when needed. You learned that hiking isn't much fun without breaks. Some of our most enjoyable times on the trails were when we found a grassy spot and took time for lunch and a nap. I loved closing my eyes on a hot summer afternoon and falling asleep to the sounds of the birds and the wind in the trees. You used to be afraid that if you stopped even for a bit, you would never start again. You no longer believe that, and I am so glad. You are showing love to yourself by pacing yourself, and this actually means your goals are reached with ease and joy.

As you hike along this trail called life, you are saying yes. You have an attitude of curiosity and openness to possible adventure as you face the twists and turns along the way. You have your eyes open for beauty and unexpected abundance on the path. You don't hold back for fear of

A LOVE LETTER FROM MY WISE WOMAN

the unknown. You trust yourself as you step forward. I know you will continue to find magic along the way.

With all my love,

Your Wise Woman

REFERENCES

Block, Peter. 2002. *The Answer to How Is Yes: Acting on What Matters*. San Francisco: Berrett-Koehler Publishers.

Block, Peter. 2008. *Community: The Structure of Belonging*. San Francisco: Berrett-Koehler Publishers.

Bridges, William. 2003. *Managing Transitions: Making the Most of Change*. Boston: Da Capo Lifelong Books.

Brown, Brené. 2010. *The Gifts of Imperfection: Let Go of Who You Think You're Supposed to Be and Embrace Who You Are*. Center City: Hazelden.

Bushe, Gervase. 2001. *Clear Leadership: Sustaining Real Collaboration and Partnership at Work*. Palo Alto: Davies-Black Publishing.

Chodron, Pema. 1997. *When Things Fall Apart: Heart Advice for Difficult Times*. Boston: Shambhala Publications, Inc.

Hoffman, Lynn. 2002. *Family Therapy: An Intimate History*. New York: W.W. Norton and Company.

Kinman, Christopher. 2000. *A Language of Gifts*. Vancouver: Rock the Boat Publishing.

Lewis, C.S. 1952. *Mere Christianity*. Glasgow: William Collins Sons and Co Ltd.

Lindbergh, Anne Morrow. 1978. *Gift from the Sea*. New York: Random House.

Merriam-Webster's Collegiate Dictionary. 2003. Springfield: Merriam-Webster, Inc.

Mohr, Tara. 2014. *Playing Big: Find Your Voice, Your Mission, Your Message*. New York: Gotham Books, Penguin Group.

Neff, Kristin. 2011. *Self-Compassion: Stop Beating Yourself Up and Leave Insecurity Behind*. New York: HarperCollins.

Rohr, Richard. 1999. *Everything Belongs: The Gift of Contemplative Prayer*. New York: Crossroad Publishing.

Vanier, Jean. 1998. *Becoming Human*. Toronto: House of Anansi Press.

www.emergingwomen.com

ABOUT THE AUTHOR

Marjorie Warkentin spent most of her working career as a nurse in a healthcare setting. As a woman who has a heart wired to care for others, you can also find her spending time giving back to her community. She has actively supported overburdened families with young children while also dedicating her time to community development and facilitating healthcare leadership development.

Marjorie has also been a trailblazer in many areas of her life, one being the main income earner for her household, providing for her husband and three children long before that was a common situation. She also started running marathons in her fifties, inspiring others to do the same. Marjorie has not let retirement slow her down. After leaving her full-time nursing career, she embraced a new role of being a speaker, author, and life coach.

Marjorie is a life-long learner with a passion for connecting theory to the practical applications that lead to transformation. With her wealth of experience and broad perspective on life, she is able to share her wisdom in accessible and inspiring ways.

In her second half of life, Marjorie is a glowing example of the life that is possible when you combine curiosity, compassion, and kindness with a willingness to be vulnerable and explore life's moments with a beginner's mind and playful spirit. She is passionate about modelling a life that can be lived with lightness and flow as she has learned to trust herself and be at peace with uncertainty.

Marjorie is a wife, mother, and grandmother who lives in Abbotsford, British Columbia.

You can learn more at www.marjoriewarkentin.com.